T0385309

ENCORE

ENCORE

ENCORE

My Journey Back to Centre Stage

RUSSELL WATSON

**HODDER &
STOUGHTON**

First published in Great Britain in 2024 by Hodder & Stoughton Limited
An Hachette UK company

2

Copyright © La Voce Touring Limited 2024

The right of Russell Watson to be identified as the Author
of the Work has been asserted by him in accordance with
the Copyright, Designs and Patents Act 1988.

A CIP catalogue record for this title is available from the British Library

Hardback ISBN 9781399738248
ebook ISBN 9781399738255

Typeset in Celeste by Hewer Text UK Ltd, Edinburgh
Printed and bound in Great Britain by Clays Ltd, Elcograf S.p.A.

Hodder & Stoughton policy is to use papers that are natural, renewable
and recyclable products and made from wood grown in sustainable
forests. The logging and manufacturing processes are expected to
conform to the environmental regulations of the country of origin.

Hodder & Stoughton Limited
Carmelite House
50 Victoria Embankment
London EC4Y 0DZ

www.hodder.co.uk

CONTENTS

ENCORE

ENCORE

VINCERÒ

THANKS TO NEARLY twenty-five years as a recording artist, I've had some extraordinary experiences. I've been to places and met people that my younger self, a lad growing up in Salford, would never have dared dream of. My success is mostly down to this thing that nestles in the middle of my larynx – my voice – and somewhat down to my personality and character. Together, they have taken me all over the world. But the voice is a delicate and sometimes mysterious thing. It demands more from me than I do from it. Illness affects it, of course. The ageing process doesn't help: it naturally deepens the voice and often lowers the range. Early in my fifties I was told that, even healthy and fully fit, I could no longer perform like my younger self – an idea that I refused to accept.

The first time I had surgery for a brain tumour was in 2006. That was bad enough. When the tumour returned in 2007, it haemorrhaged one night while I was asleep, requiring an emergency dash to the hospital. I came *that* close to dying. Psychologically and physically, my route to recovery was painfully slow, bumpy and potholed, not helped by some questionable decisions on my part. My anxiety about some aspects of my health blinded me to other aspects of my well-being, which in turn led to further problems. I didn't realise it at the time, or chose not to, but I was caught up in a potentially deadly downward health spiral. It took several years until I felt that my voice was again on song. At times I feared it might have gone altogether and I often caught myself wondering if I'd ever hit the high notes again. It was not as if I sat idle after my second brain operation in late 2007, but, in my struggle to regain form, at first I held back from finding out what my voice was really capable of and it took me a while to find my groove again. But I was determined to get my voice back to where it was before my health problems. And there was one note in particular that I wanted to once again hit: the big high B of 'Nessun dorma', Puccini's aria from *Turandot*, the opera that he left unfinished at his death.

In the early days of my career, long before my tumours and when I sang as 'the turn' in the pubs and clubs of the North West, 'Nessun dorma' was my trademark piece. By no means all of my early audiences were there to hear me sing. In fact, at times, I'd have been lucky if any of them were there to hear me sing; I was hired either as musical wallpaper or as the warm-up act for the bingo. Yet whenever I sang Puccini's aria, every time I hit that powerful, triumphant high B everyone would stop talking, look up, put down their pints, cheer, throw their hats into the air and give me a standing ovation, no matter how grim the venue. That's the power of that aria, especially that note. I've probably sung 'Nessun dorma' more often than any other aria or song, and probably more times than any other tenor. But that high note ... if you're not up to it, if you don't hit it, the magic vanishes. And in the North West, they are not shy about pointing this out.

In the past I did it with ease. People sometimes said, 'Oh my God, Russ, your "Nessun dorma" is better than Pavarotti's.'

Which is lovely to hear, but I would tell them, 'No. Way. Go and listen to Luciano. And come back and we'll have a chat. No human being who has ever lived can sing that high B like Luciano. He doesn't just belt it out; he smashes it out of the park. He's travelling on the edge of pure miracle. I don't care what anyone says – he's carved that one in stone.'

Some so-called classical music buffs waffle things like, 'Of course, it's not just about the singing, it's about the acting as well. Only Domingo generates the passion. It's got to be Domingo.'

On yer bike. Off you trot. Pavarotti's 'Nessun dorma' is unparalleled. You can argue that Placido Domingo performed it better, but the way Pavarotti's high sustained B of *'Vinceeeeerò'* rings out and sounds like he's going for a stroll along the promenade, like it was the easiest thing in the world, is what makes it unique. How he managed it is simply beyond me. Every time I hear him, Luciano reduces me to choking tears.

I used 'Nessun dorma' as the all-purpose Swiss army pen-knife of arias. If you want to whip up a stadium of sports fans, if you want to give a charity do a boost, if you want to ice the cake of any occasion, it's got to be 'Nessun dorma'. It steals the show every time. If I dare leave it out of a concert programme, I get complaints. It opened several doors for me and won me numerous contracts.

Despite the starring role of 'Nessun dorma' in my career, and my awe of Pavarotti, I must admit that over the years some of the chemistry and the tingle has gone out of my relationship with this aria. Call it overfamiliarity, but that high B can be a bone of contention. I have sometimes lowered the key by one semitone from G major to F sharp for an easier sing. This is not something I'm proud of; it feels like surrender. Many singers do it; sometimes needs must.

Ever since my second brain tumour, I was determined to get my voice back to where it was before my health problems. That big high B was, and is, important to me.

It goes deeper than that. 'Nessun dorma' is more than simply the cue for peacocking tenors to strut before bedazzled audiences, whether in a northern working men's club or in one of the great opera houses. The word that is sung – Vincerò – means 'I will win'. The character in Turandot who sings the aria, Calaf, is determined to get the hand in marriage of Princess Turandot; his failure to do so will result in his death. That sense of fighting for your life and winning is what makes the aria so universally appealing, so versatile and so adaptable. And it is particularly appropriate for me.

During my career, 'vincerò' became a personal battle cry when I was trying to overcome the challenges not only of singing but also of fighting battalions of misfortunes, some more self-inflicted than others. My full back catalogue of 'issues' is a sequence of crescendo-ing crises, including a throat operation for polyps, near-bankruptcy, two operations for brain tumours, a drink problem, addiction to sleeping pills, a heart scare and the doom-edged warnings of doctors and others that, after all I'd been through, I'd probably never reproduce my pre-tumour form.

Someone once said that success is not about how high

you climb but how well you bounce. I have the bounce-back-ability of an explosion in a squash ball factory. I've always been driven, but sometimes you have to hit rock bottom and find a place where all seems broken, futile and beyond control, before that fire in the belly is lit and you get the hunger to strive for what you want. If I began as the Billy Elliot of classical music, I have ended up more like the Rocky Balboa, endlessly hitting the floor, but rising from the canvas to make my comeback and carry the day. *Vincerò* is the recurring theme of my life.

1

MAGICAL MYSTERY TOUR

Let's back up a bit.

I grew up in a well-scrubbed, working-class family out of central casting, with my parents and sister Hayley, in Sunningdale Drive, Salford. My chief interests during my uncomplicated childhood were entirely normal: football, my bike and hanging out with my mates, part-funded by a paper round. The only difference between our house and every other house I visited in Manchester was music; no other house had classical music playing. Both of my parents listened at home: Mum, classical; Dad, country and moderate rock. The huge, chipboard-cased radiogram in the kitchen was always on. During the day, it reverberated with Tchaikovsky, Schubert, Wagner, Bach and Elgar. When Dad came home, it throbbed to Dire Straits and Johnny Cash. I hardly saw my father. He put in twelve-hour shifts six days a week at the local steel mill. I never really appreciated the distinction between Mum's and Dad's respective tastes, which may explain my love of mixing classical with other genres that has served me so well. Another musical strain in the family came from my maternal grandfather, who played the piano almost to concert standard.

My mum was very protective. She banned me from cycling beyond Sunningdale Drive until I was ten. She had two brothers with severe health problems. One had spina bifida and couldn't communicate and the other was blind and severely brain damaged at birth. I think she saw me as a gift to be treasured. Likewise, looking back I think that my grandmother saw me as a sort of blessing and she would take me everywhere given half the chance. Our family was like a cocoon.

At school, I briefly took up the piano and then the guitar. My teenage bedroom vibrated to me singing along to the top 40. I found I could mimic stars like Cliff Richard, Neil Diamond and Meat Loaf with remarkable accuracy. If I recorded myself and then replayed the cassette, I could hardly tell the difference. I thought everyone could do that. I had little idea I was doing anything extraordinary.

When I left school at 16 with one O-level in English and enrolled at Worsley Technical College, I was just as likely to be found commuting between the pub and the local hairdressing salon, where I was an enthusiastic guinea pig for the trainee stylists.

Along with my school friend Steve Gleave and a couple of mates, I formed a band, The Crowd, which sang covers of The Jam, The Beatles and The Who. I'm not sure that we were very good but we loved the music and put our hearts and souls into it. My mother landed Steve and me our first, genuine, contracted gig at Craig Hall Day Centre. Our boy duo was paid in chocolate biscuits and tea. One of the audience clearly enjoyed the show. He began furiously pleasuring himself and had to be restrained by a nurse. We were delighted that our first review stood up so well and afterwards I joked to Steve, 'Wow, I thought they would appreciate us, but not that much!'

I got a job at Sabre Repetition in Irlam, making turned parts. As a trainee, I was supposed to learn to set lathes to make nuts, bolts and washers. However I just wasn't interested and so ended up doing all of the jobs that no one else wanted to do. I hated the job. It required neither imagination nor artistic flair nor drive of any kind. All it demanded of me was a simple sequence of bodily movements above which my mind soared in dream, speculation and of course music. I was known as Minty, because I always showed up late – *after eight*. When I did night shifts, I taught my colleagues the guitar and sang them

3

Beatles songs. I left Sabre Repetition for a job making crankshafts at Hunts in Patricroft, a suburb of Greater Manchester. The job was better paid, but equally loathed.

One evening, on a pub crawl with some mates in Irlam, we staggered into the Railway Inn and stumbled on the early heats of a local talent contest in full swing, The Piccadilly Radio Search for a Star 1990, which was being played out in pubs across the North West. My mates encouraged me to give it a go. Not afraid to dream, not afraid to fail, I grabbed the microphone and sang 'Love on the Rocks' by Neil Diamond. Half-expecting to be up to my eyeballs in rotten eggs, I got the biggest cheer of the night. I won the round. Big deal. Across the pubs of the North West, four hundred other singers also got through the first round.

At that point, instead of treating it as a joke and having a laugh, I felt a switch flip inside me. I am super competitive and I like to win, a quality that I feel has been an important part of the reasons why I am still here today. And I really wanted to win this talent contest. In the next round, which was held at The Three Crowns in Stockport, the field was whittled down to twenty, including me. For the semi-final, likewise staged at The Three Crowns, I walked in and saw a crowd of about 200. I felt a tingle of excitement. Once again, I sang 'Love on the Rocks'. I made it to the final five. I suddenly realised that singing was what I really wanted to do for a living. Not only that but, in a curious way, I already felt that I had made it.

I won the final!

An agent with slicked-back hair, sheepskin overcoat, cigar and a Mr-T-esque collection of oversized gold chains and rings approached. He could offer me three gigs a week. In a major loss to the world of crankshafts, I handed in my notice at Hunts. ('We'll see you next week, then,' called out my sceptical boss). The headline in the *Manchester Evening News* shrieked, 'Piccadilly Winner Throws Down Oily Rag for Life in Showbiz'.

I found myself performing in a series of increasingly rough venues, not quite what I'd hoped for. I was soon approached by a second agent, who helped me negotiate the difficult leap from pub gigs to the more lucrative club scene. I expanded my repertoire from Elton John, Lionel Richie and Buddy Holly covers to songs from stage shows like *The Phantom of the Opera*. This slight shift towards bigger vocal performances prompted one concert secretary to ask if I'd consider operatic arias. He told me I had the voice for them. He suggested 'Nessun dorma'. *Hmm*, I thought, *I like that idea. I wonder if it would work?* After a few weeks of preparation, I tried out 'Nessun dorma' on an audience at the end of a gig. I got a standing ovation. I began to plunder the classical repertoire, much of which I already had in my head, it having been the soundtrack of my childhood.

When I began to make a living from singing, I was excitable, fresh and innocent. I felt invincible. I picked up a microphone and went for it. Forged in the back streets of Salford, my early stage persona and performance were tempered by radically unimpressed audiences. This put me in good stead. Those smoky, gritty, unforgiving venues in places like Wigan and Bolton were the birthplace, crèche and cockpit of my struggle for self-expression. They were also the scene of many priceless moments. One of my favourite memories is of a concert secretary at one club approaching the act before me, who was tuning his guitar, only to ask him what he was doing.

'I'm tuning my guitar,' he said.

'Tuning your guitar! What do you mean you're tuning your guitar? You've known about this gig for six weeks!'

Interviewed in 2001, I said I felt I was able to communicate with my audiences, and that this skill had come from working the clubs and bars. That seemed to me a far more valuable use of my time than studying at a music school. I was a good-looking young kid who probably should have been performing in a boy band. I was trying out pieces from the classical repertoire and operatic arias, and singing them pretty well, actually. They weren't perfect. I produced a sound pitched somewhere between an operatic tenor and a musical theatre singer.

*   *   *

Since I have embarked on the magical mystery tour of celebrity, whose ultimate destination is unknowable, I have found that triumph and tragedy have hedged my route with two long wavy lines. Much of the time, I have zig-zagged between these two imposters who have become like old friends, part of the very fabric of who I am. Only by being exalted, glorified, crushed, defeated, rejected, thwarted, crucified, resurrected and risen again, and only by experiencing the highs and lows, can you sing something worth listening to. Had I not had numerous medical crises, personal lapses and health scares culminating in the two operations for brain tumours that have left me without a functioning pituitary gland, I would not be the person or the singer I am now. Only in retrospect, however, have I become aware of these things, of how these experiences have made me appreciate what really matters in life and what doesn't. I'd go further and say that when I look back and see things in a wide perspective, and even when I take my own feelings out of the picture, I am still left with the abiding sense that, notwithstanding my gifts such as they are, everything of significance in my life has come about thanks to seemingly random shifts and singular moments that have leapt out of the unforeseen and either catalysed something amazing and positive, or that have opened my eyes to something drastically negative that needed changing. Where my own personal agency lies in shaping my trajectory, I don't know. I am massively driven, but by what and in which direction? My career has been flying into orbit, but, as Melvyn Bragg once asked, which orbit? I hope this book provides some answers.

2

FALSE DAWNS

MAKING THE TRANSITION from the working men's clubs to internationally acclaimed recording artist was a very difficult and endlessly frustrating progression. I spent ten years struggling in obscurity to make my career into something larger and grander than that of a latter-day troubadour.

Those early years were characterised by false dawns. So many times, when I thought I was about to shift up a gear and head off on the road to the sunlit uplands, the world would turn and I'd be back where I started, singing in the pubs and clubs of the North West again.

One such false dawn broke in the summer of 1996 when I was invited to do a run with Paul O'Grady in his Lily Savage persona. Paul had a show on at the north pier at Blackpool – or, as he put it in his high, sing-song, droning Tranmere accent, 'A Nissen hut in the middle of the Irish Sea.' Paul was the biggest star I'd ever performed with; and Blackpool is the North West's answer to London's West End.

As Paul's guest, I performed to packed houses every night for four months. My Nessun stirred up the Irish Sea and brought the Nissen hut down every evening.

Yes, I thought, *this is it! I'm on my way!* I looked up to Paul; he had an amazing persona and I was mesmerised by his ability to captivate the audience before him. I would stand in the wings watching him, learning and observing. I learnt a lot about the power of the connection between artist and audience from Paul.

When my run with Paul came to an end, however, darkness fell. Cast back into the world of clubs, I had a particularly grim time at one place as the warm-up act and trailer for the evening's bingo.

I went by the name 'Russ Watson' for my club gigs then – people only called me Russell when they were really mad at me – and I remember arriving at the club to see a poster advertising my performance on the wall saying 'Russ Watson' on it.

'Are you all right there, cock?' said the concert secretary when I arrived. 'Remind me yer name again.'

'Russ Watson,' I replied, 'like the poster up there.'

'Okay, cock. I'm going to put you on about nine o'clock. Mind, make sure you're off by 9:25, as that's when we kick off the bingo. If you're not off at twenty-five past, they'll have you. They'll lynch you, cock! What's yer name again?'

'Russ Watson.'

'Okay, cock. I'm going to write that in biro on my hand.'

Not long afterwards the concert secretary introduced me onto the stage.

'Ladies and gentlemen, may I introduce Russ Watkins!'

As I slumped in my chair in the dressing room after a particularly brutal mauling by the bingo ladies of Atherton, I thought, *God, I've sung at the end of the pier but this feels like the end of the world.* It was as if my Nissen-hut run with Paul/Lily had never happened. I felt like I had taken ten steps backwards.

There was a knock at the door. It was the concert secretary again.

'Are yer in there cock?'

'Yes, I'm in here,' I sighed.

'Do you mind if I have a word with yer cock?'

'You can have a word with my cock, but if it answers back it's going in the fucking act!'

He missed the joke . . .

* * *

Unbeknownst to me, however, at least one positive thing did happen thanks to my guest appearances on *The Paul O'Grady Show*. Arise 'Sir' Bill Hayward.

Inspired by The Three Tenors, Richard Courtice, the vocalist, had set up The Three British Tenors in the mid-1990s. He heard about me going down a storm singing the classical repertoire at Blackpool. When he found he was a tenor short for a concert at Truro cathedral in 1997, he got in touch. I auditioned and got the job. That was where I met Bill, who was The Three British Tenors' conductor and musical director.

Bill was the genuine article, a limited-edition collector's item. At the Royal College of Music, he studied under Sir Adrian Boult, the famous conductor who founded the BBC Symphony Orchestra. Well educated, well spoken, twenty years my senior, he knew music inside out, could sight-read and was fluent in Italian and French. Oh, and he was the resident organist at Shrewsbury Abbey. He wasn't like anyone else I knew. I saw him as a kind of demi-god.

Bill seemed to view me as being this silly out-of-control little boy. One of his most common refrains was, 'For God's sake, Russell . . . Oh my God . . . Bloody hell. What are you like?' There are some people with whom you know that, if the urge to crack a joke gets too strong to resist, they will laugh at you because they find everything you say funny. Bill was that person. Whereas other might say, 'What is he going on about?' Bill would say, 'Oh for God's sake Russell! You do make me laugh!'

Bill conducted the small chamber orchestra that accompanied The Three British Tenors. If the venue couldn't fit the orchestra, he played the piano. I was drawn to Bill's knowledge of the classical music that I loved.

'Have you had any vocal coaching, Russell?' he asked one day. 'I think we could do with fine tuning the instrument a little more.'

I told him that I couldn't afford his singing lessons, and that he lived too far away – his home in Shrewsbury was a two-hour drive from Salford.

'Don't worry,' he said. 'It doesn't matter. I'll do it for free.'

Once or twice a week, I coaxed my Peugeot 309 to Shrewsbury and back. Bill lived in The Old Clock Tower, a quaint local landmark. His home was laid out on five floors. I loved going there. It was always very peaceful. We would spend hours listening to his library of VHS tapes of operas. We'd trawl through videos of performances by various artists, usually tenors. He became a friend, guru and my touchstone. If I had a question about anything musical or opera-related, Bill had an answer. I look back on those times with great fondness.

When I could afford it, I checked in at the Prince Rupert Hotel, in the medieval centre of Shrewsbury, to cut down on time spent on the A49. Bill and I would spend a day and a half at his house poring over classical music. I was riveted by every word that came out of his mouth. At his piano in the basement, we'd run through a few arias together and I listened to him explaining the meaning of each piece.

I am a natural mimic and if I spend a lot of time with someone I pick up the nuances in their voice. I once rang Bill and left a voicemail message mimicking him. The phone rang out and the answering message came on.

'Hello, this is William Hayward at Dogpole Studios. Please leave a message after the tone and I will endeavour to call you back.'

'Hi Bill, it's Bill here. Get your lazy arse out of the pub and give me a call as soon as you can. I know where you are.'

An hour later Bill rang: 'You daft bugger. I've just heard your message. I had to play it twice. You sound more like me than I do.'

Give me a few minutes of someone speaking and I can pass myself off as them seamlessly. You'd hardly notice the difference. I used to do interpretations of singers too. I once did a gig at the Acton Court Hotel, a Stockport show business landmark demolished in 2010.

''Ow do you want me to introduce you tonight, Russell?' the compere asked.

'Just "Russell Watson, man of many voices".'

'Right, okay. How about this: "Russell Watson, man of a thousand voices, all of them unrecognisable"?' It did make me giggle.

Interviewed on a *South Bank Show* that was dedicated to me in 2001, Bill said, 'When I first met Russell, he was a little bit like a learner driver at the wheel of a Ferrari. He had all this power but very little control. I told him we need to get the control, so you can drive the car. It's not all about power and speed. If you are constantly focussed on belting it out all the time and burying everyone else on stage, you're going to burn yourself out.'

He was right.

We began to work on discovering light and shade in my voice.

One day, I said to Bill, 'You know all these free singing lessons . . .'

'They're on the house.'

'Yeah, but one day I'll pay you back.'

'It doesn't matter,' he said. 'You don't have to pay me back. I enjoy your company and it's a privilege to work with such a fine voice.'

'No, I'd like to pay you back one day.'

Bill had a dream. 'If ever I had the opportunity to conduct the Royal Philharmonic at the Royal Albert Hall,' he would half-joke, 'that would be like you playing for Manchester United and scoring the winning goal in the cup final. *That* is how much it would mean to me.'

We laughed at this distant visualisation of something neither of us ever thought would happen. I never for one second imagined that I'd sing at Old Trafford; he never dared think he'd conduct the Royal Philharmonic at the Albert Hall.

*   *   *

But then one day the telephone rang. The caller asked me to sing at Old Trafford, at the Eric Cantona Munich Air Disaster Memorial match in August 1998. No question, this was definitely going to be *it*. Not only would I be standing on the pitch at Old Trafford, which, as a lifelong United supporter, was pretty bloody thrilling in itself, but I would also be seen by tens of thousands. Surely this would catapult me irreversibly to the next level.

Silly me! Nothing is that simple in show business. Another false dawn was breaking and this performance fell through.

But then towards the end of 1998, I sang at a charity event at the Midland Hotel in Manchester. A few football-ers and *Coronation Street* stars were present. I finished four arias of vocal flame-throwing and exhibitionist vocal-fold oscillation with – what else? – a searing rendition of 'Nessun dorma'. On my way out, I felt a tap on my shoulder. I turned and saw a face I recognised . . .

Then it clicked: Martin Edwards, chairman of Manchester United.

'Oh Russell,' he said, 'Such a wonderful performance.'

'Thank you.'

'It'd be great if at some point, during half-time in one of the big games, you could come and sing at Old Trafford.'

'Yeah, I'd definitely be up for that.' I replied, which was quite possibly the biggest understatement I have ever uttered.

I gave him my number and off he toddled.

Time went by, and then carried on going by. The season unfolded to its near conclusion. Nothing happened. *Oh well*, I thought, *that's another false dawn to add to the collection. And did those feet walk upon Old Trafford's grass green? No, they never did.*

'Oh hello. Is that Russell?'

'Yes.'

'Oh, hello there, Russell. It's Ken Ramsden from Manchester United football club.'

I knew that Ken Ramsden was the secretary of Manchester United. I was also wondering if this was some sort of wind-up.

'Er, yeah, hello Ken.'

'We were just wondering if you might be available this weekend to come and sing before kick-off?'

'Let me check my diary.'

Fifteen cartwheels later: 'Hi, er, yeah. Turns out I am available, Ken.'

'Oh lovely. Lovely. Right, what we wanted is "Nessun dorma". Martin's asked, can you sing "Nessun dorma"?'

'Yeah.'

'And at the end, right, if we win, *if* we win, we'll be picking up the Premier League title, you see?'

'Yeah.'

'And if we lose, then we'll all just go home, to be honest with you, Russell. But if we win, can you sing "Barcelona" at the end of the game?'

'Barcelona' is the crossover classical smash-hit single that Freddie Mercury, the great front man and songwriter of Queen, co-wrote with Mike Moran.

'Yeah, course I can.'

And that was it. It was a bit like taking a booking from a working men's club, except that it hadn't gone through an agent. On 16 May 1999, I was going to walk on to the hallowed turf at the Theatre of Dreams, sing the aria for which I was becoming known, watch the match and then, if we won, give the crowd 'Barcelona'.

That afternoon, I was waiting in the players' tunnel a few minutes before kick-off. The players were still in their dressing rooms. It was just me standing beside a chap wearing an iridescent tabard. I had on my best suit, underneath which I had donned my favourite Manchester United shirt with 'Watson' emblazoned on the back. The stadium was packed. The fans were belting out 'Glory Glory', the Manchester United anthem. I got a whiff of that unmistakable smell of football crowds, a mix of beer and very cheap slightly stale cigars. The announcer came over the public address system. 'Would you please welcome, from Salford, Russell Watson, who is going to sing "Nessun dorma"!' The fans didn't quite know what to make of this announcement. Some applauded, others kept on singing. As I walked out on the grass toward the centre circle where a microphone stood, the cacophony began to die down. I remember feeling the soft yield of the grass beneath me, the first time I had set foot on this sacred turf. As the opening bars of Puccini's famous aria began to play over the loudspeakers, I took a deep breath and began to sing. During the instrumental section I removed my jacket to reveal the Manchester United shirt and cried, 'Come on you reds!' The crowd went wild.

Maybe it was because I was in Old Trafford, but when I hit *VincE-E-E-E-E-E-R-Ò-Ò-Ò-Ò-Ò!!* in front of 60,000 fans I felt like I had a connection to the universe, the most majestic, exhilarating and incredible feeling that I have ever experienced. It felt just that bit better than the best thing ever, as if Someone up there – and I've experienced this prickling sixth sense a few times – was sending something down to me that was beyond anything I could normally produce.

That high B resonated around the stadium, where as a child I'd gone to watch my heroes play and sat in the stand thinking, *My God, I'd do anything to get on that pitch.* In a flash, I felt I'd gone from that dreamy starstruck kid to David Beckham on the edge of the box, having curled one into the top corner to win the Premier League title. It felt *that* good.

I scarcely knew it at the time, but singing 'Nessun dorma' at Old Trafford gave me a pivotal moment of my career. If nothing else, as soon as Old Trafford erupted I became convinced that I was able to communicate this massively exciting and emotional so-called classical crossover music to a mass of normal people who had come to watch a football match. I came away thinking, *This is going to work.* Afterwards the local paper reported on the match, commenting, 'You know you've witnessed something special when even the cynical hacks in the press box join in the ovation. I swear even the pigeons in the roof of the stands flapped their wings when he hit the last note of "Nessun dorma"'.

United didn't do badly either. They beat Spurs 2–1. That 1999 Premier League title would be the first trophy of the Red Devils' historic treble of the Premier League title, the FA Cup and the UEFA Champions League Cup. They were the first English team to win all three trophies in the same season.

If you listen carefully to the post-match interview with Alex Ferguson, Manchester United's manager, you can hear me singing, 'Baaaaaaaacelona . . .'. It is there, etched in that moment in history for ever. That will never go away.

The following day the phone rang.

'Oh hello, it's Ken here . . .'

Manchester United had two Kens. This was the other Ken, Ken Merrett.

'. . . you went down so well. The manager loved you. Would you be available later this week to come and represent Manchester United in Europe, to sing at the Champions League Final at the Camp Nou stadium?'

Of bloody course I'm available, I thought.

'Er, yes,' I said.

That was where it all started, really started. This turned out to be an actual glorious golden dawn, thanks to my old friend 'Nessun dorma'.

After I'd sung at the Camp Nou in front of a television audience of squillions, I joined my dad on the second tier amidst the 1968 European Cup-winning side: Wilf McGuinness, Paddy Crerand, Georgie Best and Bobby Charlton. I said to Dad, 'How did we get here?' In front of us sat Alan Hansen and Kenny Dalglish, both ex-Liverpool players. How did *they* get there?

The set-up was the same: I sang 'Nessun dorma' before kick-off. With a few minutes to go before the final whistle, we were one–nil down. It wasn't looking good. People were muttering, 'Well, we nearly did it. That's why it's so difficult.' Then, I swear something spiritual happened. Two or three minutes before full-time, I looked up at the sky and thought, *Come on, just let us get one goal and, honestly, whatever You want . . .*

United scored! *Oh my God!* We were still celebrating the goal after the restart when we won an injury-time corner. Ole Gunnar Solskjær knocked in a second. Dad was jumping on me like he was my child. I have never experienced euphoria like that in a stadium, theatre or arena.

One quiet day a few months later, I sang at the Manchester United youth squad Christmas party. I was standing at reception at Old Trafford when in walked Sir Alex Ferguson, the Red Devils' legendary manager who received his knighthood in the Queen's Birthday Honours in 1999. An imposing figure, he is one of very few people whose presence makes me nervous.

'Ah Russell, are y'all right pal? Hey, don't you forget us when you're famous.' *Me forget you*, I thought – not likely!

When Melvyn Bragg kindly devoted that *South Bank Show* to me, while organising things behind the scenes the producer for some reason kept calling Sir Alex 'Sir Brian'. No one knows where the hell 'Sir Brian' came from. Sir Alex gave him one of his looks and politely told him, 'It's Alex, not Brian.' For one moment it felt like the world had stopped. Then a wry smile from the boss. No harm done. Thank you, Fergie. I last saw him at Sir Bobby Charlton's funeral in November 2023, where I sang the hymn 'How Great Thou Art'.

*   *   *

This time, it felt like momentum was finally building. It wasn't going to be another case of a golden opportunity followed by radio silence. Now was the time to make things happen. As an urgent, some might say impetuous, young tenor, I decided that one way I might be able to do this was by sending a CD to David Bryce, Cliff Richard's tour manager. I had no specific plan. Still giddy from the highs of Old Trafford and Camp Nou, and more convinced than ever that what I offered was valuable, I thought it was worth a try. I had recorded a CD in a small DIY studio in the rafters of my friend Alastair Gordon's house. I sang over backing tracks to 'Nessun dorma' and 'O sole mio'.

Amazingly, as I'm sure David Bryce got sent millions of CDs, he rang back.

'Cliff's in rehearsal at the moment. Can you come down to his studio?'

I caught the train to London.

At the appointed address, I found a converted church. Entering, I saw David Bryce locked in talks with another man. Noticing me, both stopped talking and gave me a look that said, 'Who the hell is this guy? Security!'

David Bryce introduced the other man as Clive Black, making it abundantly clear that Clive was the son of a famous writer and lyricist, Don Black. I had heard of Don through his collaborations with John Barry, one of my favourite composers, famous for his film music. I was in the presence of showbiz minor royalty.

David showed me to an office.

'Is this you, m'boy?' He flourished my CD.

'Is what me?'

'Is this you singing on here?'

'Is it . . .?'

'Did you sing all this?'

'Yes, I did.'

'So it's you.'

'Yeah, it's me,' I said, slightly confused. Then the penny dropped. 'Ah, okay, fair enough. I know what you are thinking. It's a CD. Could be anyone's.'

'No, no, no, m'boy. No, no, no. NO.' Well, yes.

'Tell you what,' I said, 'let's just go through into the recording area.'

We got up and walked out of the office and into the large expanse of the main body of the converted church. I sang 'O sole mio' a capella and, as I did, Bryce's jaw went into freefall.

'Just a minute, m'boy.'

He called Cliff.

The next thing I knew, I was being driven to Bray Studios, where Cliff was rehearsing for his Route of Kings tour. I'd never seen anything like the set-up at Bray. Cliff was standing on a massive, fully lit stage singing: 'It's so funneee, how we don't talk any more.'

The music and everything else stopped. Cliff walked over.

'Er, hi Russell,' he said. 'It's nice to meet you. David said that you've got an amazing voice. And you're gonna sing "Nessun dorma" for us this afternoon.'

'Yeah, that's right.'

'Take it away, Russell. Let's hear it.'

So I sang 'Nessun dorma'. After I hit the high B and the aria had finished, Cliff stared at me, eyes wide open.

'Er, when d'ya wanna start, Russell?'

Back of the net!

On the Route of Kings tour, in 1999, I was introduced as the Next Big Thing to a crowd of 25,000 Cliff fans in Hyde Park. Over the three concerts, I sang to a combined audience of 75,000. Later, I did nine concerts with Cliff at the National Indoor Arena in Birmingham. At 10,000 fans per concert, that represented an audience of 90,000. While my mind whirred with numbers, my mother was thinking that headlining with the living embodiment of the menopausal hot flush was the best thing ever.

All thanks, again, to 'Nessun dorma'.

One outcome of the Route of Kings tour was the outstanding job it did of raising my profile. Among the people who heard me sing was Elaine Paige. She later passed my name on to Mike Moran (who would eventually become my pianist), saying, 'You've got to hear this guy. He's amazing.'

3

SALFORD ICARUS

MY BRUSH-FIRE SUCCESS at the close of the 1990s prompted Decca, the world's pre-eminent classical music label, to give me a five-album deal. I wanted to appeal to as many sets of eardrums as possible. Just as in the clubs where I'd seen people sit up and listen to music they didn't know they liked, I wanted people who didn't see themselves as classical music fans to listen to it and think, *Yeah, actually, there's really something in this opera stuff.*

At the time, I had a predominantly female audience that I could reach fairly easily. In classical opera, the tenor is always the romantic hero, while the baritone is the baddy and the bass is the dad. The tenor either gets the chicks or dies in the attempt. So I knew I was going to be packaged for female consumption. I also wanted to appeal to a broader audience, including your typical bloke who likes a game of football and a pint on a Saturday afternoon, your man's man if you like. I wanted him to feel completely comfortable having my CD lying on his coffee table, so that he could play it to his mates, and say, 'He's all right, 'im, Russ. He's one of the lads. He's pretty cool.'

This was my brief to my first manager, who I engaged around this time. He rose to the challenge. Enthusiastic, energetic and very, very forceful, he was a true believer; he was convinced that, with his help, I'd become the greatest star in the world. He was good at dreaming up off-the-wall ideas that provoked reactions like, '*Seriously?*' He excelled at 'making shit stick', a technical showbiz term.

One such brainstorm was to team me up with Shaun Ryder, songwriter, poet and former badass singer of Happy Mondays, the Salford rock band. Shaun then was a top-of-the-range, old-school hell-raiser with a tabloid half-life. This provoked welcome outrage: 'Shaun Ryder and Russell Watson? That is the most unlikely combination ever!'

Our finest hour as a duo was recording 'Barcelona', which we put together and released as a single in 2000. 'Barcelona', a collaboration between the soprano Montserrat Caballé and Freddie Mercury, is a landmark in the classical crossover genre. In its production it was agreed that, were a song to be written, Freddie should sing as a rock singer and Montserrat should sing as an opera singer. Neither should compromise the other. The song would represent the best of both the rock and opera worlds. Its intertwining of rock and opera styles defines and provides a template for the entire classical crossover genre.

Nick Patrick was my producer for mine and Shaun's recording. Ever since 1991, Nick had been one of the behind-the-scenes pioneers of so-called 'Classical Crossover'. He has produced albums with some of the biggest classical names. He is always a joy to spend time with.

When Shaun and I arrived at the recording studio, Nick turned to me and said, 'Mate, why don't you, erm, head off back to the apartment and come back later? I'll record Shaun. You pop back in a few hours when we are done, okay?'

'Sure.'

A few hours later, I returned to find Nick and his assistant sitting in the studio, twiddling their thumbs and spinning on revolving chairs.

'How did it go?'

'Well, erm, yeah, we got a few bits, mate,' said Nick. 'But then Shaun literally pulled his headphones off and said, "I'm sick of you two Wrangler-wearing fucks. I'm off to the pub."'

Shaun's streetwise, colloquial, raw, let-it-all-hang-out approach meant that some of the material he'd recorded was unusable. Indeed, not all Shaun Ryder on the finished track of 'Barcelona' is Shaun Ryder. I had to mimic him when recording his ad libs – *The music vibrates me-e-e-e*. I think he'd cleared off to the pub by then.

Although I didn't fully appreciate it at the time, if I listen to our version of 'Barcelona' now, I can hear that it is a work of genius. It sprang from the chaos in Shaun's mind when he was not yet on the wagon.

Our visit to the city of Barcelona to shoot the video was the biggest, non-stop laughter-and-piss-taking goofball trip. Everything that is mad, bad and irrational in crossover music was taken to its ultimate doomsday scenario in this pop and opera classic.

In June 2000, Shaun and I were booked to perform 'Barcelona' on *TFI Friday*, the Chris Evans show. Shaun had previous on *TFI*. Much of what fell out of his mouth struggled to clear the profanity filter and was certainly unbroadcastable before the watershed. In light of a particularly colourful earlier appearance on *TFI*, Chris Evans had pleaded with Shaun, 'Now, when you come on, please Shaun don't swear, okay? We're going out live.'

'Yeah, sure Chris, no problem. Don't worry. I promise I won't swear. I'll be a good boy.'

On the day, Shaun walked out before a live audience wearing a pair of flamboyant brogues. Chris looked down. 'Oh wow! I like those shoes, Shaun. Patrick Cox?'

'Course they fucking are!'

After that, Shaun had to be pre-recorded.

So Shaun and I performed our act in the afternoon before the live show. Behind us was a full band, including eight attractive women playing violins, violas and cellos, a rock guitarist, a drummer, backing singers, disco lights, flaming sconces and enough dry ice to re-launch Concorde.

Our duet took me to a new level, and off in a new direction. My manager had been right on the money. Shaun gave me cred, which was my aim. He was an important catalyst: all the big television shows clamoured to book us; he put my name and face in front of the pop music press. The *New Musical Express* lavished a centre spread on us. Headlined 'The Dirty Divos', the article featured a picture of me immaculately suited, hair all coiffured, while Shaun wore his signature hat, baggy trousers and tracksuit top. The writer cooed that the combination of our voices was ahead of its time. No other classical artist has ever made it to the centre spread of *NME*. I wish I hadn't lost my copy of that issue.

Shaun has been through it all – still *is* going through it all – but he remains a legend. Shaun Ryder today is a mellower beast than the one I knew. His rampant hedonism and constant disarray seemed to go hand in hand with a wild creativity. Lightning flashes of genius would crackle out from beneath the maelstrom of his life.

The release of 'Barcelona' was the first time that I felt that things from then on would be different. I wasn't going back to the clubs and bars. There would be no more false dawns. My life was about to take a dramatic turn. My career would translate on to a higher plane.

*   *   *

When putting together *The Voice*, my first album, I wanted to include Shaun's and my 'Barcelona' because my rendition of this song at Old Trafford had been a big catalyst. I obviously couldn't have left off 'Nessun dorma' even if I wanted to, nor 'Panis angelicus' and 'Funiculì, funiculà' – big numbers that went down well in the clubs. I added some crossover classics, 'Nella Fantasia' by Ennio Morricone from the film *The Mission*, and 'Caruso', a brilliant piece that Lucio Dalla, the singer-songwriter, wrote in 1986, inspired by the last days of Enrico Caruso, the great Italian tenor. 'Caruso' was one of the most requested songs whenever I performed on television shows. I then tossed in some of my favourite pop songs, 'Bridge over Troubled Water' and 'Vienna'. For me, *The Voice* was my *Desert Island Discs*-in-waiting; for the listener, I wanted it to be a joining-of-the-dots, so that he or she could appreciate the connection between different styles of music and perhaps realise a bigger picture in which the distinctions between different genres become at best irrelevant and at worst obstructive. There are only two types of music: music you like and music you don't like, and I think that's all subjective.

When *The Voice* came out in September 2000, it sold 36,000 copies in its first week and stayed strong in the charts all the way to Christmas, battling it out with Robbie Williams and Lionel Richie. It just kept selling and selling and selling. I almost couldn't believe it.

I look back on each of my albums as if they were my children but with licence to judge. *The Voice*, my first, has never been equalled never mind bettered. Forget about sales, I'm talking excitement and newness. It felt like magic.

I say 'forget sales', but I'd be lying if I said that I didn't care at the time. Seeing it rise in the charts and knowing that people were walking into shops and swapping their hard-earned cash for the album I had yearned to make was a wonderful feeling.

After Christmas, Dickon Stainer, head of Decca, rang.

'Christmas week?' he said. 'Have a guess.'

'No idea.'

'One hundred and ten thousand, Russell.'

This had never happened before. *The Voice* became the best-selling classical album of all time in the UK. I was on every television show, every chat show. (Between

2000 and 2010, I sold more albums in the UK than Madonna.) After ten years, I had become an overnight sensation. *Encore*, my second album, outsold *The Voice* in the UK, but *The Voice* sold more worldwide. The least perfect of all my recordings, *The Voice* remains my favourite because of its innocence. People who don't normally listen to classical music connected with something about it and loved it.

The more albums I sold, the more the purists among the classical music critics responded with a wailing and gnashing of teeth. They queued up to attack.

Ohmigod, he's from Salford! ... Wait, where is that? ... Not quite our aria, darling ... His records will bomb ... He's a flash in the pan ... He won't last five minutes ... He's a fad ... Elevator music! ... Warn us next time – sick bag too far away ... He's generating a lot of noise ... Well, he has to, darling, otherwise the people trying to flee the auditorium won't hear it.

The *Telegraph*'s opera critic likened me to a 'karaoke crooner'. I didn't mind the 'crooner' bit, but, given that the musicians on the album were the Royal Philharmonic Orchestra and that it was recorded at AIR Lyndhurst studios in London, one of the top recording studios for classical music in Europe, the 'karaoke' bit was perhaps disrespectful.

Some of the classical music critics seemed outraged

that a precious bit of their elite personal culture was being pimped up, mass-produced, packaged and peddled to the mass market. Their sense of exclusive ownership and entitlement to classical music meant that they hated and despised what I was doing. The critics regarded me as something between a laughing stock and public enemy number one. The more they went for me, though, the more the record-buying public seemed to go to the shops.

The classical music industry basically falls into two groups of people. In one group, there are people who think they know everything about classical music; in the other there are people who think those in the first category are pretentious twats. They are not absolutely separate categories, however. The long border that they share has plenty of places for crossing under cover of night, but you can guess which side of the border the critics generally prefer to stay. It is just as well that not everyone, including record labels and the public, believed the critics. Anyway, they were from a world that I wasn't interested in, never have been. Well, sort of.

Up to a point, the critics were right, of course. I was nothing like the finished article. My early albums were nowhere near the level of technical accomplishment that these guys were used to. When I listen to my first recorded version of 'Nessun dorma' on *The Voice*, I think,

35

My God, that note is all over the place. Some of the Italian is wrong: the rounding off of the vowels is not quite right.

In those days, I sang Italian phonetically. I didn't speak Italian. I simply learnt the sound of the words. We had an expert in Italian in the recording studio and if they said, 'No, he's not got that word quite right,' I would record it again.

However, the many flaws of *The Voice* were part of its popular appeal. If the critics scoffed and others felt threatened, I saw myself in more Promethean terms, bringing light to benighted areas. Looking back, I now see that *The Voice* was selling into a pre-existing market that had already been defrosted, warmed up and brought to the boil thanks largely to The Three Tenors.

When the recording of The Three Tenors concert at Italia '90 became the best-selling classical album of all time, it came as a wake-up call. It was time for a new feeling in music. The general public's view of classical music was changing.

I'm sure that when planning the 1994 World Cup in the United States, someone sitting in an office somewhere thought, 'Blimey! That music that they used in the 1990 World Cup went down well. Let's do it again.' So The Three Tenors squeezed back into their white tie and performed a concert in Los Angeles for USA '94. This went a long way further to popularise what I'd call core classical music. Meanwhile, coincidentally, I was belting out the same classical repertoire to growing numbers of fans in the North West.

Some parts of the music industry were suddenly abuzz with distant horizons, vistas of possibility and sunny tomorrows. Others, however, seemed curiously short-sighted and slow on the up-take. While my album *The Voice* was in gestation, I was surrounded by all these very clever people at the record label who knew what they wanted. I knew what I wanted, based on my experience of what did and didn't fly in places like Bolton and Wigan on a Saturday night. I often found, however, that my tastes diverged from those of many people whom I met in the music industry. Some of their ideas were preposterous. I had much to learn about many areas of the industry, but I thought that this new-ish hybrid genre and its rapidly growing market had, at least until I came along, somehow eluded some – but not all – of the high-ranking executives. I remember thinking at the time that the music industry advances one P45 at a time. I'm not saying I was responsible for the classical crossover boom in the UK – I was following a blazed trail – but I helped take it in a new direction.

If you look at what the music industry was trying to do at the time with stars like Nigel Kennedy, Vanessa-Mae, Charlotte Church, Aled Jones and Luciano Pavarotti, it was packaging them in a user-friendly way for general consumption. Vanessa-Mae was promoted as an attractive young woman playing the violin. Nigel Kennedy was presented as a trendy young bloke who liked his football. But it was still classical. None of them were adding in the energy and sounds of pop music. You would never have heard 'Nessun dorma', 'Bridge over Troubled Water' and Ultravox's 'Vienna' all on the same album. I was the first to take classical crossover where it truly belongs, music for everyone. My manager then threw a bit of fairy dust on top of it by teaming me up with Shaun Ryder. Others have since piled in.

The late Michael Parkinson, the chat show host, once said to Bill Holland, MD of Universal Classics & Jazz, 'You need to look after this lad Russell Watson. At the moment, he is in a queue of one. No one has the versatility to do what he does.'

That queue of one rapidly grew to a long queue of singing crossover schmaltz, movie soundtracks, pop-opera and souped-up classics with the boring bits taken out, often presented with star-spangled production values of glitzy lighting and shiny-floor staging.

Others spotted the opportunity. Although it didn't feel like a movement at the time, I can now see in hindsight that it was. Some of those artists that came on were really good and some enduring talents have emerged.

What constitutes classical crossover today and what it ought to sound like is up for debate and a moving target. But it is not nothing and it does matter. It seems to be going through a dip due to lack of new ideas. What I do know, however, is that we live in a musical rainbow environment. Music hasn't got more complicated, but the public's appreciation of what it does and doesn't like has grown more sophisticated. Today is the first time in history that so many different types of music, from easy-listening lounge music with lush orchestral textures via pop, country, folk, rock and R&B to scary avant garde, have passed the old grey whistle test and are now featuring on our playlists, in our living rooms and in our headphones at once. There is no such thing as bad music, only different kinds of good music.

Now, besides the occasional needling, the classical music critics leave me alone. The hornets nest has moved on.

As it turned out, vilification from the stuffier quarters of the music establishment probably did my sales a lot of good. Freddie Mercury was right: 'Stuff criticism, darling, I'm bringing classical opera to the masses.' As it turned out, attacks by the critics were the least of my problems.

39

4

ROCK 'N' ROLL

'Good evening, Wembley!' I said into the microphone.

There was a moment of silence.

'Get on with it!' shouted a bloke in what counted as the audience. It seemed the very thin crowd in The Phoenix in Ellesmere Port that evening had failed to appreciate my sense of humour.

'You know what?' I answered back, 'if I'd've known there would be this many of you here, you could have come back to our house and I'd've put on the show there.'

The Phoenix was an old brick building so called because it had burned down a couple of times and been rebuilt. To reach the stage, you had to climb up the fire escape, a flight of steep metal steps that zig-zagged up the outside of the building.

I'd begun the evening, as I did most evenings, by opening the boot of my battered, fifteen-year-old Peugeot 309 parked outside my two-up, two-down council house, and

41

filling it with two PV sub-bass bins, which were massive – four feet wide and three feet deep – an amplifier that weighed a ton, a box of wires and a few clumps of tumble-weed for company in case it was a quiet night. Once I got to The Phoenix, I had to drag all that lot up the fire escape. It was a Sunday night, dark, cold and hammering it down.

I was my own sound engineer. I set everything up myself. Typically, on any given night, I would do my gig, collect £70, pack all the gear away into my car, drive home and get to bed some time after 2am. That was my typical working day. Ah, the delights of shoe-string show business!

Once I'd got myself set up that evening at The Phoenix, at around 8pm, the concert secretary came over.

'Ey, yer all right there, lad? I'll stick yer on about nine o'clock or something like that if that's all right with you, mate.'

'Yeah, that's fine. Whenever you are ready.' I looked up and saw an empty bar. Sensing an all too familiar tumble-weed moment, I asked, 'Er, does it fill up?'

'Might get another couple in, mate, but it's a Sunday. It's been dead the last few weeks cos the weather's shite.'

'There's two people in.'

'Yeah, we won't even bother doing bingo. At least you're gonna get paid, arenchyer?'

'Yeah, I suppose so.'

At nine o clock, I walked on and made out three people standing by the bar. In such situations, I used to switch on to autopilot and treat the evening as a rehearsal. So I stepped up to the mic, tried on a few light jokes, did my night and went home. It was just one of many, many gigs I did around the North West at that time – some good, others bad, a few totally unremarkable – I didn't give that evening at The Phoenix a second thought.

Fast forward three years to 2001, and I walked out on stage in front of a full house of 11,000 people at Wembley Arena. Behind me were the combined forces of the Royal Philharmonic Orchestra and a twenty-voice choir. Outside, touts sold tickets at three times the cover price. As soon as the lights hit my face, I took the microphone from the stand and shouted out euphorically, 'Good evening, Wembley!' Just for a second, my mind leapt back to that miserable Sunday night at The Phoenix in Ellesmere Port with its three hapless bystanders for an audience. In a dizzyingly short space of time, I'd gone from *that* to the strange lifestyle of a megastar, having everything done for me and not having to lift a finger other than to order another drink. I looked up to the heavens and said, 'Thank you'.

Working the clubs and pubs of the North West was a fantastic learning curve for my future career as a performance artist. Some of the audiences were wonderful; we had some great nights. Others were less wonderful. I look back on that period and think, *God, that was hard.* Then I reflect, *I would not be the performer, the personality or the entertainer I am today had I not had those early formative years and that background.*

* * *

Things began to move fast. Once I made the shift from singing in pubs and clubs to becoming a recording artist following the launch of *The Voice*, the public couldn't get enough of me. There was less, 'Get on with it!' and more, 'Let's get it on!'

Already 33 when *The Voice* came out and I ascended into the limelight, I had some catching up to do. The following three years were more, shall we say, rock-and-roll than classical opera. As I saw it, that was part of the deal. Having grafted hard over the previous decade, I felt I had earned the right to be a licensed loose cannon. Needless to say, I didn't stop to consider how rarely that ends well. There was partying and flinging music stands out of hotel windows. Well, not quite, but we'd certainly tear it up. Some of the nights out were, in the context of Decca, the music label for whom Pavarotti had been legendary.

The first three years of my career as a recording artist were the most insanely driven and neurotic time of my life. The frantic timetables, the complicated flight schedules, the thrills, the spills and the highs were exhausting. I never said 'no'. It was as if I had to do everything that came my way.

Even if I said, 'I need a break,' my manager would say, 'Yeah, but this has come in.'

Then more would come in off the back of that. I was like a machine rolling faster and faster. It was the maddest, craziest, most amazing, exhilarating phase of my career, a rollercoaster ride of wild excitement.

* * *

I also found that I was beginning to be taken seriously by music royalty. In autumn 2000 I was about to sing in a musical tribute to Jill Dando, the television presenter gunned down outside her house in Fulham in April 1999. I was in my dressing room when there was a knock at the door.

'Hey Russell!'

It was Lionel Richie, who was also appearing in the show. Lionel and I had crossed paths before, usually in corridors behind the scenes at shows.

'Hi Lionel! How are you? Come in. We'll have to stop meeting like this.'

45

'Yeah, the circumstances this time are tragic. But I saw your name on the door and thought, *It's Russell again!*'

We began to chat. I mentioned that I was planning a second album and that it would be great if we sang a duet together.

'You know what,' said Lionel, 'I got this song that I sang with Pavarotti. I never released it as a record. It is called "The Magic of Love". That would be great for us to do.'

'Okay, let's do it.'

Our duet appears on *Encore*. That is how you get to do a duet with Lionel Richie. Just keep appearing where he is appearing. It was a lesson in how show business works. Had I approached him cold, I would probably have been turned down. It is much better to be asked than to ask.

Watching Lionel in rehearsal, I could tell from the way he interacted with everyone around him that he has the same respect for everyone no matter who they are. An absolute gem of a man, Lionel is the epitome of a gentleman, a superstar and an all-round lovely human being.

* * *

Success in the UK is one thing; success in the States is something altogether different. There was no single high-water mark, just many large waves for surfing.

When I first performed at Carnegie Hall in 2001, *The Voice* stood at number one in the US classical crossover charts – a not insignificant achievement since it represented weekly sales of 30,000 to 40,000 records. I was ranked among the top one per cent of UK exports to America, even outselling Robbie Williams in the States. At the same time, I was also number one in the UK.

That evening, I stood in the wings of Carnegie Hall while the brilliant Boston Pops Orchestra boomed out the opening bars of 'O sole mio'. I walked on stage to a packed house and began to sing. Very quickly, the place erupted. People began clapping and cheering. I thought, *Holy shit! So this is America!* I'd never experienced a roar of appreciation halfway through a piece like that night at Carnegie. I thought, *Hang on! This is just the start! I haven't finished yet!* I felt like I'd hit the crest of a massive wave. I never knew such a feeling was possible.

My arrival in New York seemed at times almost surreal. If I so much as put one foot outside the Trump International Hotel, there'd be a stretch limo with plasma televisions screens and a bar waiting to take me to interviews on *The Rosie O'Donnell Show, Good Morning America* and *The Today Show.*

For Larry King, I sang 'Va, pensiero', also known as the 'Chorus of the Hebrew Slaves' from Verdi's *Nabucco*, which involves singing in two different styles of voice.

'My Gaad,' said King, 'when you did that thing when you sing like a pop singer and then all of a sudden there is this, like, explosion and this operatic voice comes out from nowhere . . . I just couldn't believe it. It was right on the money.'

In November 2001, I made my West Coast debut at the opening of the Kodak theatre (now called the Dolby Theatre), where the Oscars are held. I was the very first artist to perform in the theatre and the whole of the Hollywood glitterati turned up for the opening. By that time, Bill Hayward had become my musical director. I was delighted to have him with me. He conducted the Hollywood Bowl Orchestra, another dream come true for him.

Variety magazine commented, 'Russell Watson puts over the pop material more convincingly than any of the moonlighting opera singers or even pretenders like Michael Bolton who go the other way.'

When we got back to the UK, my manager insisted I had a corps of bodyguards around me, muscle in suits.

'Seriously?' I said.

'Guard of honour, Russ,' said my manager. 'Important for your prestige.'

Everywhere we went, my way was cleared by a cool-enough flying squadron of tight-suited Praetorian floor-walkers in mandatory dark glasses.

Mr Watson is coming through!

At the Classical BRIT Awards at the Royal Albert Hall, four suits rode shotgun.

Make way, Russell is coming through.

Meanwhile, Decca was treating me like a finely tuned racehorse. The attention to detail was unrelenting. *Everything* mattered – the songs I sang, the shows I performed in and the way I looked. Different people from different departments, wardrobe, hair, make-up and styling, were all over me. Everything had to be immaculate: suits, initialled cuffs on the shirt, diamanté cufflinks, tie knotted with no gap between knot and collar, and the button on the top collar elasticated so that when I sang it stretched rather than choked me. My shoes were polished so that I could see my future in them ('Oh, those are just cracks in the leather, Russell'). My hair was coiffured to perfection; my make-up was a piece of artistry. I even had an on-road stylist. Everything was perfect! I was born to run and win.

Those days felt like I was in a different part of the universe to the back-street working men's clubs of the

North West where I earned £70 a gig playing with Fred on the Hammond organ and Bill on a four-piece pearl drum kit in the corner, in front of audiences of between three (3) and one hundred (100) punters, depending on whether *Coronation Street* or the bingo was on that evening. The early noughties were a brilliant time for a lad from Salford; they were also a very, very bad time to be a person with limited willpower other than a single-minded determination and drive to succeed.

*   *   *

I can't resist sharing one particular story about my time in America. It relates to the time I was invited to sing at the Trump Taj Mahal (now the Hard Rock Hotel & Casino) in Atlantic City as part of a big programme organised and broadcast by the PBS network. I performed in front of a huge audience alongside Lea Salonga and Natalie Cole and a brilliant orchestra.

Donald Trump found out about the event and his people contacted PBS, who contacted my team and asked if we would be happy if he were to introduce me onto the stage. We said that we would of course be delighted.

Now before these events performance artists and their teams are normally sent a rider – showbiz speak for a document that the performer sends back, summarising their requirements for the performance. My mates travelling with me and my team decided – with some encouragement from me – that it could be amusing to send back a hilarious list of requests. So, we duly replied, requesting that my dressing room should be stocked with bowls of M&Ms – but with the green ones removed – along with two blow-up dolls (one brunette, one blonde) in opposite corners of the room and helium-filled condoms. The cherry on the top though was my friend Alistair Gordon's request for a 'gusset typewriter'.

'What on earth is that?' I said to Alistair.

'I've no idea and it doesn't matter,' he replied. 'Let's see what they come up with.'

So the appointed day came and we duly arrived at the Trump Taj Mahal and were shown to our dressing room, where we opened the door only to find all of our requests carefully met! There in front of us were two blow-up dolls, bowls of M&Ms (without the green ones), helium-filled condoms and – *yes, really* – in the middle of the room an old-fashioned 1930s-style typewriter, with a pair of tights on top of it.

'That must be the gusset typewriter!' said Alistair.

Just before the show there was a knock on the door. It was Trump himself, coming to say hello. He was accompanied by a girlfriend, whose eyes nearly popped out of her head on seeing the contents of the room. Trump however was not at all fazed and didn't even flinch.

'Nice to meet you, Russell,' he said. 'So how would you like me to introduce you tonight?'

* * *

I called Bill 'Sir' William. He's neither a baron nor a knight of the realm; he's neither MBE nor CBE nor anything that merits a title other than 'Mr'. 'Sir' just seemed to suit him: he was very well spoken and the sort of character that you would be very unlikely to meet as a kid growing up in Salford. He was a different animal to anyone that I had previously met. He didn't speak like me. He didn't present himself like me. He was a middle-aged former school teacher and he was everything that, at that particular time, I wasn't.

The 'Sir' handle soon caught on. Producers, managers, recording technicians, instrumentalists and sound engineers began to address him as 'Sir William'. The States fell for it big time. Bill took me to one side one day and said, 'You know, Russell, America is bloody amazing. They are treating me like a king. It's wonderful.'

Three days after we arrived in New York, Kevin Gore, president of Universal Classics Group, rang me:

'Russell?'

'Yeah, hi Kevin.'

'Hey, man, er, yeah, I just wanted to check something with you?'

'Yeah.'

'Sir William.'

'Yeah.'

'He's, like, the real deal, yeah?'

'As in . . .?'

'Like, he's a knight of the realm. He's a Sir.'

'No, no, no. It's just a term of endearment, an affectionate term.'

'Fucking hell, man! We booked him first-class flights on Virgin Atlantic, the best suite in the Trump International and he's had literally everything poured on, man. He's had a stretch limo picking him up from the airport.'

Bill's regal treatment ended abruptly. The red carpet was rolled up. His room was switched from double penthouse suite to single room, fire-escape view. The iced champagne, the fruit and flowers and the keepsake bags were whisked away. His flight home was downgraded to economy. One wonders if, somewhere in Manhattan, an ennobled but hapless guest of Universal Music Group (which owned Decca) was slumming it in a broom cupboard, flying economy and strap-hanging around Manhattan.

Touring the States, Bill and I concocted my greatest

'hold my champagne' moment. It occurred when my fame in the USA reached its zenith.

In June 2001, I was invited to join several big-name American artists to perform before President George W. Bush and Laura Bush in an 'American Celebration' at Ford's Theatre in Washington DC – the historic spot where Lincoln was assassinated. After touching down two days earlier in order to rehearse with the Boston Pops Orchestra under Bill Conti, who scored the *Rocky* movies, I had been struck down with a very bad sore throat. My manager called a doctor, who prescribed the strongest off-the-shelf drugs available.

'You gotta complete the full course of medication and avoid alcohol, okay, buddy?' said the doctor.

'Yeah, okay.'

Drugged up, I made the rehearsal. My first piece was 'O sole mio'. Normally, when rehearsing with an orchestra, the conductor goes *tap-tap-tap*, whispers a few words and exchanges a knowing aside with the first violin. Not Conti. He mounted the podium, waved his arms about, and it was as if he had hit the button marked *Ker-boom!*

The sound practically blew me off the stage. It was note perfect. I was convinced I was hearing a recording. When I glanced over my shoulder, the orchestra was sawing away. Even the brass were straight on it, horns and everything, right on the button. I've never seen a conductor work an orchestra like Conti. He was brilliant.

When it came to 'Nessun dorma', though, the horns made a mistake.

'What the fuck was that?' cried Conti, breaking the golden rule among conductors never to eyeball the horns, who, by the nature of their instrument, have a tough enough job without being shouted at by the conductor. 'I could play that better myself and I can't even play the horn.'

We made it through the rehearsal. The performance was a glittering black tie gala attended by several senior politicians from both main political parties, as well as Cabinet Secretaries, White House Chiefs of Staff and Joint Chiefs of Staff. Thankfully my throat survived the performance, just. Disaster averted. Afterwards, the artists lined up in a guard of honour for the Presidential couple.

'That was fantastic!' said Bush, shaking my hand.

We got chatting. 'What you up to at the moment?' I had the presumption to ask him.

'We are coincidentally about to go into Europe,' said Bush, trying to break off my shoulder. 'We will start by going into Holland and then we drop into the UK as well. That's about it. You know, Russell, you should come aboard Air Force One and sing for us!'

'I'd love to but I can't. I'm busy myself at the moment.'

The President gave me a look. 'You're . . . What do they say in England? You're cheeky! That's what you are. Cheeky!' The following day I got an invite to sing at a luncheon that the First Lady was planning to host at the Watergate Hotel.

From Washington I flew to New York for some television appearances. On my arrival in New York, the head of Universal hosted a dinner at a high-tone restaurant. Bill and I were invited. Still on the throat meds, I forgot, or possibly ignored, the injunction from the doctor and began drinking this stupidly expensive vintage Krug champagne. After only a couple of glasses, I felt very drunk, as if an alien had entered my body. I enjoyed a drink, but I normally remained disciplined and *sotto voce* when 'on business'. Out of nowhere, I began messing around, telling jokes, singing and talking nonsense. I've never felt so off-my-face on such a small amount. Unfortunately, my doomed attempt at cross-cultural musical and comedic appreciation failed to hit the right notes. What in the north-west of England might be regarded as 'qualities', in uptown Manhattan were seen not merely as flaws but as grotesque character defects. I didn't spot the eyeballs careening sideways. I was out of control on a lethal cocktail of vintage Krug and throat medication.

Bill read the room.

'Russell,' he stage-whispered. 'I think we ought to go.'

The doorman whistled a stretch limo out of thin air. Bill joined me in the back.

As soon as the limo began nosing its way through the mad swirl of Manhattan streets, I decided to have a WWE-style wrestling match with Bill in the back of the car. 'Russell, you daft bugger. What are you doing?'

When we rolled up outside Trump International Hotel, a liveried porter pulled open the limo door, tumbling Bill and me unceremoniously out of the car and on to the sidewalk outside one of the most prestigious facades in New York City, where we lay in a heap, like that scene from *Arthur*. I remember looking up at the doorman and thinking, *I expect he's seen worse but I can't be certain.*

I stood up and yelled, 'Wa-haaayyyy! Come on Bill! Come on mate!' I began ruffling Bill's hair.

Entering the lobby of the Trump International, I managed to convince Bill that I was now on best behaviour. I promised I would no longer be a nuisance.

As I uttered these words, my eye caught sight of a pair of large double doors to one side of the lobby that were open. Beyond them, some kind of party seemed to be in full swing.

'Hey Bill! Look! There's a party! Let's go to the party! Come on!'

That evening something strange had gripped me.

We made for the double doors to the party, where a waiter held a tray and stood sentinel.

'I'm sorry, sir, this is a private party.'

'Private party?' I said. 'We *are* the party!'

'It's Mr Clinton's fundraiser.'

'Oh yeah, I know Bill. We're good friends. Bill's invited us.'

'Er . . . er . . . .okay . . .'

'Bill and I are like *that*,' I said, waving two hands with crossed fingers. 'We go back years. Go and get us a bottle of Dom Pérignon, would you, pal? And two glasses.'

Instead of bouncing us out on our ears, the waiter went off and, much to my surprise, came back with a bottle of champagne. I swept into the ballroom like a whirlwind as if I owned the place, and went through everyone without a care in the world. A four-piece band was playing jazz numbers. I went up to the pianist.

'We're on next,' I told him, as I mounted the stage.

'What?'

'I said, we're on next.'

'No, we're booked for the night, man.'

'No, you're not. We're here by special request from Bill Clinton.'

Looking baffled, the musicians began to make way. I turned to Bill.

'Sir William!' I called out. 'Come on! We're on!'

'What are you doing, you daft bugger?' said Bill.

'We're on now. We'll do a couple of songs.'

'I've not got any bloody music.'

'You don't need any bloody music and neither do I. Get up and we'll just play.'

'Play what?'

'We'll start with "O sole mio" and finish with "Volare".'

'You're off your bloody rocker.'

'I don't care. Go on. Get up.'

Having commandeered the stage, I called out to the room: 'Right, we're here by special invitation of Bill Clinton, everyone. We need a bit of order. Can you be quiet now?'

Everyone began looking round. Smooth, hard, marmoreal double-breasted men and sleek, padded-shouldered, impossibly coiffured women looked up as if a lunatic had crashed their party. Many wore expressions of 'Who or what the hell is this?'

'Come on, quiet. Oi, you at the back! Shut up!'

The room began to fall silent.

'Right, are you quiet now? Cos I think you're gonna like this!'

I sang 'O sole mio'.

When I belted out the final note, everyone began yelling for more. The musicians in the band, who had sat there looking utterly flabbergasted, leaned over and said: 'Wow! Oh my Gaad! I'm so sorry, Mr Watson . . . We had no idea. That was amazing.'

The entire room joined me in singing 'Volare'.

By the end of our act, the room was in a state of shock and awe. Bill and I were carried off stage on the shoulders of fundraisers, donors, handlers, pollsters, roadies and hangers-on, and spent the rest of the night quaffing Dom Pérignon, socialising and being the centre of attention.

If I'm performing something for the first time, doubts sometimes lurk in my mind. *Will the audience like me? What will they think? Will anyone criticise me?* That evening, I had no doubts. When I mounted that stage, I had not a care in the world. I knew that everyone would love me, and that it would be amazing. And it was. I was on fire.

The string of scenes that evening from the restaurant, to the limo, to falling out of the limo, to breezing into the ballroom, seems almost a dream-sequence or a scene out of *The Mask*, the film starring Jim Carrey about a man who finds a magical wooden mask that transforms him into a zoot-suited green-faced troublemaker able to alter himself and his surroundings at will. My personality that night cut across every aspect of who I normally am. I would never usually dream of doing what I did. Something in those tablets combined with the champagne temporarily turned me into a rampaging rapscallion that I quite enjoyed but also found scary. I wish I'd been more like that character more often, but I liked my own personal space and didn't get much of a kick out of social events. I was shocked to think I contained that 'other' person.

It turned out that Bill Clinton wasn't even present.

Meanwhile, the costs of my hedonism were . . . well, I never even stopped to consider them. Unbeknownst to me, they were mounting up.

5

HANGING BY A CHORD

IN THOSE DAYS money proved a very steep learning curve. The way it worked was that I received an 'advance' against future sales in order to fund the production of an album, and then another payment when the album came out. For *The Voice*, that further sum was £90,000 – an almost unbelievable amount. Not only that, *The Voice* was profitable. This was a situation that seemed too good not to abuse.

When I entered second-album territory in 2001, I thought, *Great! Let's go to America. Let's rent a beach house.*

I went with my team to Long Beach Island, New York, where we set up a studio in a six-bedroom beachfront villa. Not too shoddy, eh. We proceeded to drink every nearby liquor store dry of the finest champagne, all paid for by me. The making of *Encore* was the biggest boys' holiday of all time.

One problem with wrapping oneself up in the rock-and-roll lifestyle, as I soon discovered, is the cost. All those limos, bodyguards, cases of fizz and beachfront villas have to be paid for, and it certainly isn't the record label that picks up the tab.

Call it hubris or the arrogance of negligible experience, but, by the time *Encore* came out in October 2001, I'd already pre-squandered the money that I was hoping to make on future sales. Presented with an 'unrecouped balance', I had to make another album in order to recoup the balance that several weeks of carnage in a beach house in America had blown apart. I was spending money like it was going out of fashion – and sure enough, it did.

There was another deeper, darker more costly situation evolving.

In the first three years of my career, the main benefactors of my success were the record label, my management and lawyers.

Desperate for my fifteen minutes of fame while trying to move on from my pubs-and-clubs phase, I became involved with a management company who offered what seemed a good package, wage, car and a passport to larger stages. *Yeah! Where do I sign?*

The deal had its advantages in terms of security, but, for a career that advanced as rapidly and as far as mine, that security felt like a shrinking cage.

I consulted a law firm to help extricate me from my contract. Meanwhile, I took on another manager. A meeting was set up with the old management to hammer out a settlement. They offered to settle. 'If you pay us back the £70,000 we have invested in you, we'll call it quits'.

In those days, £70,000 seemed like a huge sum. I'd never experienced anything like it. Instead of settling, I was advised to fight. Big mistake. After one year of litigation, I had little to show for legal bills of £125,000. I engaged another firm of lawyers. Three years and almost three-quarters of a million pounds later, the dispute remained unresolved. I dropped that firm and hired a third set of lawyers. Twelve months and a six-figure sum later, the case fell apart and never went to court. I never recovered a penny of the money I had spent on legal fees.

Meanwhile, my finances seemed forever to defy transparent depiction. My own company ended up being in massive debt. Saving £70,000 cost me nearly £1 million. Much of it went straight into lawyers' pockets.

By the time I launched *Reprise*, my third album, I was nearly bankrupt. I'd been performing to packed venues; I'd sold millions of records all over the world; I'd pulled in between £3 million and £4 million. I had a brilliant time. But I never got rich.

I did a few back-of-an-envelope sums. If you've got 15,000 people filling the Manchester Evening News Arena paying an average ticket price of £70, that's £1.05 million gross. Normally, the artist would expect to receive half. If you have twelve such concerts a year and another twelve the following year, and then add in appearances around the world, you should be earning a bob or two. I wasn't. By the end of 2003, I had huge debts in tax, VAT and God knows what, and a bin full of final demands. You can try running from that sort of debt, but you can't hide.

I look back on those years with a wry smile, but I always have to stop myself and say out loud, 'You had no idea what you were getting yourself into!' My early career both as a recording artist and as a stage performer provided many salutary lessons, not least in music industry finances and in knowing whom to trust and whom to listen to. Among many life lessons, the most important was: never empower any agency, management firm or record label to have complete control over everything that you do. This is what I let happen. It was my fault. My hunger for success blinded me to the small print. In many cases, there wasn't any small print.

By 2003, I was in a state of total impecunity. Broke, scared, angry, I blamed everyone but myself. I felt let down. As soon as I saw what had happened, as soon as the blinkers fell off, I thought, *Oh God! How has this happened?*

My meeting with the Inland Revenue, the banks, accountants and other creditors to discuss an Independent Voluntary Arrangement (IVA) was among the most embarrassing moments of my life. I looked around the room and saw lawyers and account-ants all with their hands out. These people who'd been smiling at me and saying how well I'd done were not smiling any more. I had a choice: go bankrupt and suffer the guilt and shame of carrying that stigma to my dying day, or radically amend my life and claw my way back to solvency. My accountant suggested bank-ruptcy. Me being me, I told my accountant, 'No, I don't want to be known as the bankrupt Russell Watson. I don't want that tag. I want to pay back every penny I owe.'

Besides my overdue beginner's course in music industry finances, I also received a harsh lesson in how very easily bad luck seeks out those deep in debt, and how one problem rapidly compounds with another to create a third, far greater and more intract-able problem.

* * *

Meanwhile, while I was firefighting lawyers and grappling with difficulties with managers, unbeknownst to me at the time another problem was gathering momentum, of a far more serious nature, and which with intractable hindsight I trace back to a concert at the M.E.N. arena in 2002. On the day, my throat felt sore. I considered cancelling but baulked at the costs, costs I could ill afford. My manager, as ever, pushed hard. He always referred to counter-parties as 'victims'. Anyone who entertained us on business was a 'victim'. Sometimes I felt I was the real victim.

'Okay,' I said, 'I'll give it a go.'

I survived the majority of the programme. When it came to 'Nessun dorma', I pushed so hard that I felt like I had sheared off the surface layer of my vocal folds. At the end, I practically had to be stretchered off. I heaved a guarded sigh of, if not quite relief, then the sort of exhaled 'phew' that you make at the end of a horror movie. It was hell, you are covered in sweat, but you made it through without organ failure.

Within a few days, I had forgotten all about the concert. My voice sounded fine. Or did it? My falsetto wasn't quite right. Of course, I went into denial. A few weeks later, while recording Reprise, my friend Alastair Gordon, who was helping produce the album, noticed something unusual in my voice.

'Hey Russ,' he said, 'there's a crack in your falsetto?'

The slightest flaw in the folds affects the voice, especially in the upper register where the oscillation is at its greatest. Singing falsetto, my voice sounded like a small piece of machinery grinding away without oil. A specialist at Wythenshawe Hospital diagnosed vocal polyps, tiny blisters which had appeared on the vocal folds. I would need an operation to fix them. Vocal polyps commonly occur when a singer fails to look after his or her voice. No matter how tiny, the slightest lump, flaw or abrasion on the folds will affect your singing voice, especially in the falsetto register. For example, a song like 'Bring Him Home' from *Les Misérables* is impossible to sing with polyps since it demands a lot of falsetto.

The enormity of my predicament hit me like a hammer blow. I'd just learnt that everything I assumed was real was not real. All the money that I thought I'd made had found its way into other people's pockets. Despite my success, I had no financial gain to show for it. I had lost everything I'd made. Now, I was facing a risky throat operation. If it went wrong and somehow damaged my vocal folds, I would be left with neither singing voice nor further career, which, compounded with my financial plight, meant that I would be staring at oblivion. This realisation was one of the scariest moments of my life.

Back home, heartbroken, I lay curled up in the foetal position whimpering and praying to every deity I could think of. If I lost my voice, that would be it. Career over. I might as well put my head between my legs and kiss goodbye to anything I could still reach. Everything that I'd achieved would vanish, beginning with the repossession of my house, which the banks were already eyeing up. I'd be back cutting bolts. Within three years, I had gone from a trail-blazing megastar to a cautionary tale.

I also felt, slightly perversely, that, were I to complain, people would think I was a moaning, whingeing bastard. Ostensibly, I had this incredible career and an amazing life. If I spoke out of turn, or let it be known how low I felt, I'd imagine people screaming, 'Oh my God, there he goes again. If I had that life or that money, I wouldn't be feeling like that.'

I began to bottle things up. The only people I discussed my financial affairs with were a few close friends. I knew, however, that no amount of well-intended guidance would ransom me from my situation. The only thing that would save me was my voice.

The decision as to which surgeon to choose to remove the polyps was one of the most critical of my life, especially as you cannot insure vocal folds. Preying on my mind was a similar operation that had gone wrong for

Julie Andrews, causing temporary loss of voice. After going to great lengths, I lit upon Philip Jones at the Department of Speech and Language at Wythenshawe Hospital in Manchester.

Mr Jones and I discussed many aspects of singing. He'd seen me perform a few years earlier. We got along. I thought, *I like this man; I think I trust him.* His reputation and track record sang out clearly.

The next question was whether to have the polyps removed by laser surgery or manually with a knife. Jones was abundantly clear on this point. He cautioned, 'Laser did for Julie Andrews. I wouldn't recommend it. Were I to perform laser surgery on, say, Jim the bricklayer who has a polyp, he'll emerge saying, "My throat is fine". If I'm operating on Russell Watson, internationally renowned tenor with millions of record sales, that is different. There is a huge responsibility. I must make sure I do the best possible job.'

So we went ahead. Jones excised the polyps manually with a surgical knife.

As part of my recovery, I took a vow of silence for several days. Of course, I couldn't resist creeping downstairs to the hall one day, like a naughty school boy, and giving the voice a try. I sang one note using my falsetto range.

Clear as a bell.

'Oh my God!' I stage-whispered. 'Oh my God! I'm reconnected to the universe, never mind my career and possible future income stream!' I had a little cry to myself.

Before the throat operation, with spiralling debts and my voice cracking, I had faced my darkest hour. That I found Mr Jones, who had weighed the risks and proceeded with manual removal not laser surgery, and that the operation seemed to have gone well, struck me as another meaningful coincidence, a get-out-of-jail-free card. My vocal folds were vibrating properly and healthily in a literal sense, but also vibrating high enough in a spiritual sense to connect me to the powerful energy of the universe. I had gone from feeling like a total write-off to feeling unstoppable once again. Well, that is how it seemed.

A few days later, I visited Mr Jones for a progress report.

As he sat in his chair, he said, 'Russell, do you mind if I say something?'

'Go ahead.'

'I went down your throat and, I have to be honest with you, I've never seen anything like it. You literally have the Arnold Schwarzenegger of vocal folds. They are incredible. The infrastructure down there is amazing. I've never seen anything like it.'

72

Good to hear. Nevertheless, had the operation not gone absolutely to plan, it would have been 'hasta la vista, baby' and not 'I'll be back'.

In the end, my house was not repossessed. I managed to sell it, but the bank took the profit. I moved into modest rented accommodation in a beautiful area in Sale.

To the outside world, it may have seemed that from 2000 to 2003 I was one of the biggest and richest stars in the world, packing out arenas and punching out a sequence of number one hit albums. The reality was that I didn't own a car, had no money and was now living in rented accommodation.

Some people rise to the occasion in a crisis; others sink into moral decrepitude. For the next four years, for every £3 I grossed, £2 went to pay off arrears of tax and debt, as well as the monumentally large lawyers' fees that I incurred while trying to extricate myself from various asymmetrical contracts with third parties.

A few years later, debt-free, I was in Selfridges department store on Oxford Street inspecting the watch counters. Behind me I heard, 'Hahahaha! Russ-ell!'

I turned round and saw a face from my past.

'You can't afford that, can you?' jeered the face.

I looked the face in the eye, and said, 'I can now that

I'm not with you f*****s any more'. I turned and walked off.

You need neither qualifications nor any measurable skill to become a manager in the music industry. Anyone can walk their dog down the street one day, and say to themselves, 'Hey, why don't I give it a go?' If you stumble on the right talent, have a semblance of credibility, and have a basic knowledge of how life works, you too can manage a musical act. Welcome to the last bastion of the unemployable. You could say the same of me. No one would have walked into Sabre Repetition in Irlam or Hunts in Patricroft thirty-five years ago, seen me joking around, trying to shirk twelve-hour night shifts and mimicking my line manager, and said, 'One day you will be the UK's best-selling classical vocalist.' Whichever way you look at them, most careers in the music industry are improbable. No one knows whom the industry will next love and choose to be famous. It has a secret alchemy all of its own.

Looking back, it is tempting to apportion blame to everyone except oneself. I realise that my financial problems were largely my own fault and no one else's. I let them happen. I ceded far too much control. I was utterly naïve in business. Many factions around me saw me as easy pickings. I'd left school at 16 still a child. I was playing toy soldiers with my sister when I was working on the shop floor in Salford. That childishness continued into my early thirties. A positive factor when I was a child, the protective bubble that my mother created around me at home meant that when I stepped into adult life I was clueless. I only left my parental home in my mid-twenties. It beggars belief how naïve I was in the first four years of my recording career. I had to grow up very, very fast.

6

FINE TUNING

WHEN HE AND I first met Bill Hayward told me that too much of too much is heading for disaster. And this is why professional singers whose livelihoods depend on consistently attaining the very highest standards need a vocal coach close by at all times. Bill travelled with me whenever I went on tour. If I erred, or if he spotted something amiss, he'd say: 'You need to be careful there, Russell. You're pushing too hard. You need to rein it in. Lighten that particular passage.'

Bill could be very prescriptive. For 'O sole mio', for example, he would say there are certain bars where I should go light to rest my vocal folds in readiness for the really big notes, which would thereby make a greater impact.

I began to pay careful attention when preparing for each. If nothing else, my pre-concert routine gives me confidence. Sleep is essential. If I've slept well, I can look in the mirror just before going on stage, and I think, *Hooh! Yeah! Looking good tonight.* I walk on feeling confident. If I have an interrupted night, I will do everything in my power to sleep during the day, lying in until 3pm if necessary. My throat and vocal folds operate best when rested, relaxed and hydrated. On the day of a concert, I drink so much water that it's swishing around inside me like the English Channel. On stage, I keep blueberries to hand to hydrate the vocal folds. A superfood rich in vitamin C, blueberries stimulate the saliva glands, which helps to stop the mouth getting dry. I never set foot on stage without blueberries.

Before a performance, I used to eat Jelly Babies for energy, until someone pointed out that sweet things produce mucus that sits in your airways. Dairy has a similar effect. Coughing to clear the mucus agitates the folds, which impairs the voice.

Some people might be surprised at how little singing practice I do. If I have two gigs either side of two days off, I won't sing or practise on those two days off. Nor do I take vows of silence. Some vocalists press the backs of their hands to their foreheads, cough lightly into a linen handkerchief and say, 'Please don't speak to me, darling. I need complete vocal rest.' That's not me.

Voices need loving care and attention. Any form of bellowing, screeching, shrieking and yelling is a menace to the vocal folds, which is another reason why it is important that I get the testosterone levels right and keep a few Joni Mitchell tracks handy just in case. If I drop in on the Cleric Stadium near where I live to watch Congleton Town of a Saturday afternoon, I guard against getting overexcited, no easy matter when the Bears play at home.

So I avoid shouting, which is not always easy. I've anger-managed myself down to the occasional gruff retort, and I'm thinking of giving up altogether. Walking the dog, I whistle. To make me shout, you'd have to present me with overwhelming evidence that are you are an absolute twat.

I shun confrontation and, if things get fiery, I'll put my coat on, slam the front door – my most strident form of protest – and get in my car, slam that door, and go for a drive, which I find helps put things into a different perspective, and often ends up with me saying to myself, 'God, how pointless was that? Now, I need to do this and that. I should call so-and-so, and make sure I get all that sorted out.'

If I ever do accidentally shout out loud, I go, '*Oh my God! I shouted! There, I've just shouted again! Help! I hope I haven't injured myself.*'

If I've not sung for a week, I will go into the hall two days before a concert and do some scales to make sure

79

the Arnie of vocal folds is in working order. Then I will run through one of the bigger pieces. If I can nail a big number like 'Nessun dorma' straight out of the bag, I'll leave it there, reverberating around the hall. I won't practise any more. I know that I don't have to worry about the performance two days later.

Common sense would say that common sense would break through where matters of vocal health are concerned and one's livelihood is at stake. Life, however, is rarely common-sensical and never that simple. When you reach the upper echelons of fame and stardom, you hit an inflection point where everything becomes inverted, nuanced, intricate and often conflicted. Vanity and the temptations of sycophancy often trump the best intentions of vocal coaches.

How did I sound?

Oh darling, you were amazing! No one has sung 'Agadoo' quite like you did! Absolutely wonderful! Which is code for: can you renew my contract please?

More recently I have turned to voice coaches if I felt I had a problem or was slipping into bad habits or wanted to brush up on my vocal reproduction, burnish an aspect of performance technique or simply improve something purely stylistic.

Singing requires a skilful blending of art, science and physical fitness. It involves being aware of, and taking control of, several muscle groups that we all use during the course of breathing and talking but without thinking about it. Mastering your breathing is essential. It is extremely difficult to do this without a vocal coach. Once you have a handle on the technical aspects, you then have to learn almost to discard them or at least consign them to your muscle memory so that you can concentrate on connecting emotionally with the song and not just focus on the notes. The number of variables at play when trying to sing professionally is endless.

The only snag is that one voice coach will almost always flatly contradict the next.

Decrease the space on the last note . . .

No, no, no, no. You need to open up the space on the last note.

I'm interested in what works. I'll take advice, go away and try it out. If it works, I'll stick with it; if it doesn't, I won't.

While my early albums struck a chord with millions of fans, the priesthood of experts and classical music critics who savaged my technique made me, and some at Decca, think that perhaps my voice needed fine tuning. Paul Moseley, a 'creative' at Decca, put me in touch with Patrick McGuigan.

A distinguished baritone whose CV as an operatic performer ticked off Sadler's Wells, Glyndebourne, the

National Opera and Kent Opera, Patrick juggled teaching positions at leading institutions with teaching
some of the great and the good. An alchemist of the
voice, Patrick could turn gravel and sandpaper into
gold and silk. He was good on the technicalities of
singing. Most importantly, he could explain them in a
way that rarely provoked the response, 'What on earth
is he on about?'

Stuck out in the wilds of west Cheshire, Patrick's
timbered, wood-beamed cottage near Northwich had a
decent-sized garden at the back. Whenever I dropped in,
I always thought, *This is the type of place I'd like to end
up.* A side door led directly into his sitting room. In a
corner stood a piano, a record player and a cassette
recorder. One wall was dedicated to vinyl; another to a
library of sheet music of a scope and amplitude I'd never
seen before.

I told Patrick I liked to sing crossover music including
the pop repertoire, and that I wanted to avoid veering
too far towards the classical operatic style. While some
of the criticism I had received had stung, I refused to let
it alter what made me me.

'If I tried to perfect that type of classical technique,' I
said, 'I'd risk losing everything that makes me what I am
as an artist, whatever that is. I specialise in the stack 'em
high end.'

'Of course, Russell,' he said, in his soft southern Irish brogue. 'I completely understand your position in the marketplace. We don't want to go too . . . purist. I don't want to change what you do because what you do is completely natural. I want to improve your technique but not over-coach you. You are already naturally doing most of the things that I would want you to do.'

This sounded promising. I liked Patrick already.

While he put me through a tough warm-up, *La-la-la-la-la-la*-ing my way up and down the scales, Patrick would tune in to my voice, analysing it like sonar. Within five minutes, he'd have me up to B flat. This was a more tiring, higher-volume approach than I'd learnt before with other vocal coaches.

'Right,' Patrick would say. ' "Vesti la giubba." '

While 'Nessun dorma' is the most famous of the classical tenor arias, it is not the most difficult. 'E luce-van le stelle', for example, one of two great arias in *Tosca*, is a monster. Perhaps the most brutal is 'Vesti la giubba', which falls at the end of the first act of *Pagliacci* by Ruggero Leoncavallo. This piece starts high, contin-ues high and finishes high. It is right up there, bump-ing along the ceiling of the tenor's range. Every note sounds like a dare. There's nowhere to hide. The string of consecutive high As demands great stamina and control. Queen, the rock band, used the climax of this

83

aria in the opening lines of 'It's a Hard Life', which reminds me, once again, what a remarkable vocalist Freddie Mercury was.

'Vesti la giubba' will rarely have audiences on their feet. It hasn't the dynamics of 'Nessun dorma'. But it is a hell of a sing. Performed well, it will drill anyone to the bottom of their soul.

'I get goose bumps just thinking of Mario Lanza singing it in the 1959 film *For the First Time*,' I said to Patrick. 'Lanza was one of Pavarotti's favourites; mine too.' The brilliant operatic heart-throb tenor who starred in MGM movies in the 1940s and 1950s, including *The Great Caruso*, was also one of my mother's favourites.

'Me too,' said Patrick, 'Much more attention needs to be given to Lanza's genius. Too easy to sell him short. I'm sure we could have a lively discussion about how all the great tenors approached this aria.'

'In my opinion,' I said, 'Luciano Pavarotti doesn't sing it as well as Placido Domingo, but he certainly makes it sound effortless.'

'Well, Russell, perhaps you've put your finger on *why* you prefer Placido. Luciano sings it, but does he *live* it? This aria is about emotional pain. The character of Canio discovers his wife's infidelity just as he is due to go out and perform as Pagliaccio the clown. Can you imagine how he felt? The aria has to sound difficult, painful and anguished. The technical challenges are part of its identity.'

Vesti la giubba literally means 'wear the jacket' or 'on with the motley', i.e. the show must go on, the great industry rallying cry. Sharp minds might further adduce that an aria that dwells on the psychological problems of a clown is a pretty apt reading of my career.

'Right, Russell, let's hear it then.'

I'd sing:

Recitar! Mentre preso dal delirio
non so più quel che dico,
e quel che faccio!
Eppur è d'uopo, sforzati! . . .

Which translates as:

Act! While in delirium,
I no longer know what I say,
or what I do!
And yet it's necessary. Force yourself!

I finished the piece red-faced and fighting for breath.

'How do you feel?' asked Patrick, smiling and nodding.

'Yeah,' I gasped, 'tired.'

'Exactly! You are giving it too much. Now, the thing with these types of pieces, Russell, is that the *tessitura* – that's the range of pitches in a melody or vocal part, from the Italian for "texture" – is very high. So you have to treat it almost like a vocal obstacle course. If you go off hell for leather at the start, you're going to be exhausted by the middle, and you won't get to the end. So we have to find a way of getting from A to B, from B to C, and from C to the finish . . .'

As Patrick spoke, I momentarily lost myself in the sheer musicality of his soft, lilting baritone.

'. . . and so that is what we've got to do,' said Patrick. 'You have to maintain your balance throughout the performance. You can't go in like you do with a lot of the big arias. You won't get through it.'

That is how we worked. He'd let me make a bollocks of it, and then explain why. In helping me find my way through the vocal obstacle course, Patrick helped me discover the commando within. I became a tougher, more strategic version of myself. He became my number one go-to vocal coach.

I bounced out of that meeting feeling exhilarated. Besides being a vocal coach, Patrick seemed to fit the template of mentor that Bill had carved out. I don't deliberately seek out friends who are older than me, but I appreciate their wisdom, knowledge, experience and intelligence, and I always hope that some of it might rub off. This might be a reaction to my sudden awareness of my naïveté and its costs.

I respected Patrick. For a while, I saw him two or three times a week, and learnt a great deal very quickly. He showed me methods and ways around certain arias that made their singing more manageable. Every time he showed me a new technique, I couldn't wait to get on stage and try it out. I felt like he was showing me a fascinating new land of discovery.

*　　*　　*

Besides his deep understanding and warm sympathy, Patrick embodied another important quality: positivity. I'm a big believer in the power and value of positivity and positive people. If I'm feeling flat, a friend like Alistair Gordon can lift my mood within five minutes of meeting him. A fantastic singer in his day, Alistair played keyboard in Zu Zu Sharks, the 1970s New Romantic band. Now in vocal production, he is the most rock-and-roll human being I know. They just don't make them as rock-and-roll as Alistair any more. No matter when, where or how, if Alistair shows up, the party begins. He has the constitution of an ox. If Grant Ainsworth, my long-suffering sound engineer, and Alistair get together, chaos ensues.

We sit in the hot tub, and laugh, drink and talk nonsense. When the sun rises, we're still spouting nonsense at each other over the last flatness of the champagne, by which time my stresses, doubts and problems will have melted away. It's hard to explain what makes these sessions fun, but they always are. Whatever is said in the hot tub, stays in the hot tub, to be resumed on our next 'evening of grand*ure*', as Alistair puts it. More often than not, a bedroom is prepared for each guest. The following day, bleary-eyed, we arrive one-by-one downstairs in the kitchen for coffee and an assessment of the damage. Usually, the one who claims the loudest to be up every morning at seven no matter what is the one who doesn't surface until well after lunch.

These guys share my philosophy and outlook on life.

Another positive radiator, Josh Abbey was my recording engineer on *Encore*. A typical Noo Yorker, Josh sports a big moustache, slicked-back grey hair and an easy-going, wisecracking charm, *like y'know*. Every now and then he'd get really animated and then he'd get *fuckin' animated*. He'd be, like, *Y'know what the fuck, Russell. How can you let these people do this to you, y'know? You need to do somethin' 'bout this!* And then he'd sink back into his normal, meek, mild self. He's one of the nicest, purest human beings.

Later, after my second tumour operation, Josh said, 'This is Russell. This is his life! It is up and down. It won't ever stop. He always seems to find a way through. He is a fighter. He is the Rocky Balboa of the music industry.'

It's funny he should mention Rocky. As a child, I was a massive fan of the *Rocky* series. *Rocky* and *Rocky 2* generated so much pathos and still do. Whenever I watch them, they open up memories of childhood and remind me how fragile life is. Sylvester Stallone, who plays Rocky – or is it the other way round? – was criticised for his acting, but if you watch him in *Rocky* and *Rocky 2* he is phenomenal. You become totally invested in the character. You can see that he really meant it. There isn't a shred of irony, winking or inverted commas about his portrayal. By *Rocky 5*, Rocky has lost all his money. Knocked down, he gets back up, gets beaten, goes back in, and next time round wins the fight. When I saw that film, I thought, *Hey! That's me! I was a nobody from nowhere, just like Rocky. My life is a Rocky-style slugfest!*

When Josh said I was the Rocky of the music industry, I thought, *Well, I'm not on as grand a scale as Rocky, but the ups and downs are the same. I have his resilience and positivity.*

7

THAT'S LIFE!

By 2006 I was fully debt free. Meanwhile, Decca decided to release a greatest hits album. No need to sing a note. No need even to visit a studio. It was just a question of energising the back catalogue. On release, sales went through the roof and the album soared to platinum. Throughout its first week, I was fighting it out with Corinne Bailey Rae, who had launched her debut album. Having traded positions for the top two slots all week, she pipped me to number one by a tiny handful of sales. I was back in the higher echelons of the charts again, all over the TV, and was fast becoming one of the BBC's poster boys. My career was back on track.

But all this time, while my life and career seemed to be alternately exploding in some directions and then imploding in others, I began to feel unwell. For at least two years low energy and mood swings had made me suspect a breakdown or some kind of depression. At times I felt a pain in my head that was beyond extreme, as if someone had plunged a dagger between my eyes. My sight deteriorated. Watching television became agony. I would go to my bedroom, close the curtains and lie and wait and hope and try not to cry. Having my eyes gouged out with a plastic spoon and my teeth removed with a rusty hammer would have felt like blissful escape. Thinking I was suffering with migraines, I became almost addicted to naproxen.

In 2006 I booked an appointment to see a doctor at a BUPA clinic in Manchester. It was late one afternoon when I arrived at the near-empty car park. The doctor clearly couldn't wait to go home.

'It sounds like stress,' he said. 'It's nothing. Have you had a holiday?'

'No,' I said.

'Maybe try a holiday.'

'Really?' I asked.

'Yes. It sounds like stress.'

I emerged from the clinic more confused than ever. What I did know, however, was that the pain was still there. Six months later, my head still hurting, still thinking it was migraine, I flew to Los Angeles to work on my fifth album.

The plan was to record at Capitol Studios in the Capitol Records Tower in Hollywood, the famous one that resembles a pile of stacked discs. Frank Sinatra, Nat King Cole, Michael Jackson, Dean Martin, the Beach Boys and many other American greats had produced legendary albums here. Accompanying me was Nick Patrick, my producer.

The low cabin pressure on the flight from London seemed to worsen my condition. I had never experienced such pain before. I felt like my body was being invaded by torturing demons. Besides the headache, my peripheral vision had shrunk to the size of a ten pence coin. Arriving in Los Angeles, I said to Nick, 'I can hardly see.'

'Mate, you just need to get out,' said Nick. 'Let's have a game of tennis. Clear the cobwebs away.'

We went out on court at the Beverly Wilshire. Nick hit a decent shot to my backhand. Watching the ball clear the net, I swung and . . . missed. The ball simply vanished. I looked behind me. There it was, laughing at me at the back of the court.

'Must've been the speed of my forehand, mate,' said Nick, uncertainly.

I needed to get myself checked up – not my backhand; my head.

Meanwhile, we had work to do. Recording began. I was going to work with Gregg Field, Frank Sinatra's last drummer, as well as several of Frank's old brass players, and Tom Scott, the saxophonist, composer and co-founder of the Blues Brothers. These guys were at the top of their game. It was a pure privilege to record with them.

A couple of days into the project, we went out for an evening. It was one of the weirdest nights. I felt completely detached from everything. Normally I'm cracking jokes, chatting shit, drinking and generally being a dick. But I sat there thinking, *What the hell is going on? Why does my vision feel like it's closing in? Why does my head feel so cloudy?* I felt like I was literally not in the room.

The following day, without telling anyone, I slipped out of the recording studio and made my way to Cedars-Sinai, the big hospital in Los Angeles. I took a general optical test, a pressure test on my eyes and then a visual field test where I had to peer into a machine and press a button whenever a dot appeared. I sat there for ten minutes waiting for a dot to appear. 'When are you going to switch on the machine?' I asked.

'Er, Mr Watson, we already did,' said the nurse. 'The machine has been running for several minutes.' I had failed to spot every dot in my peripheral vision.

I was summoned to a specialist's office and sat down in front of him. In a monotone voice, he said, 'Mr Watson, you have a tumour. From the results I'm getting here, I'd say it is a big one.'

I felt like I was on a movie set of a film, in a scene where the character floats out of his body and objectively sees himself sitting in a chair. I saw the shell of my person being talked to, but failing to take anything in. I snapped to. As the doctor continued talking to me, I thought, *Yes, I knew this would happen.* As a kid, I'd had this recurring dream that always ended with a massive explosion in my head. I had also had this inner feeling that something catastrophic would happen to me on the dawn of my 40th birthday. And here I was on the dawn of that birthday.

For the first time, I felt my mortality threatened. It was scary. It was made scarier still by being in a foreign country with no family around. I didn't want to ring my family and worry them unnecessarily.

Unnoticed, I slipped back into Capitol Studios.

That evening, I stood on my balcony on the seventh-floor of the Beverly Wilshire, taking in that famous flaming Los Angeles skyline at dusk. I was in such screaming, red pain that I thought for a fleeting moment about jumping. Anything to stop the excruciating pain in my skull.

I managed to reel that thought back in though, thankfully.

Three days later, back at the Sinai, I had my introduction to the 3-D horror that is the MRI scanner, a massive, noisy machine like a scene from a *Star Wars* movie.

95

I asked the specialist, 'How long will I be in there for?'

'Twenty minutes.'

After what felt like twenty hours, I was extracted from the machine.

'Er, Mr Watson, we didn't quite get everything we wanted so we're just going to pop you in there for a short time again, if that's okay?'

'Yeah, all right. Fair enough.'

They reinserted me for another twenty minutes. By the time they pulled me out, I was sweating and feeling stressed to the eyeballs. My heart felt like it was a furious prisoner pounding against my ribcage to get out. Just as I thought the stress could get no worse, a giant man approached wielding a needle attached to a tube containing what looked like blue dye.

'We're just gonna put a drip in you, Mr Watson. It contains iodine. It will colour the blood vessels so that, when we put you back in, it will help to show up the images better.'

'Hang on a sec,' I said. 'You've already had me in there for forty minutes. What more do you want?'

Then the doctor who had done the MRI scan came out and said, 'Mr Watson, we are just going to put you back in for a short while.'

I clearly had a frustrated film director on my hands. I came this close to saying something regrettable.

'You know what? I've been in there forty minutes. I'm sure you've got enough pictures by now. I'm not going in again, I'm out of here.'

It turned out that they did indeed have enough images to confirm the diagnosis: I had a brain tumour.

Somehow, while in Los Angeles, I managed to finish recording the album. Title: *That's Life*. Almost equally incredibly, I managed to conceal the diagnosis from my colleagues, fellow musicians and family.

*   *   *

I managed to avoid telling my family about my tumour. I didn't want them to worry, especially my mother. I knew that the operation to remove the tumour wasn't going to happen overnight. First I had to choose a surgeon; then I had to finish putting together *That's Life*; and then I had to put various affairs in order. I didn't want my family to worry about something for three months when they only needed to worry about it for twenty-four hours. Naturally, when I broke the news to my parents and sister, they were upset.

The worst bit was telling my daughters. Rebecca was eleven; Hannah, five. I was living in Hale at the time. It was the children's bedtime on the evening before I was due to head down to London and go to hospital. I'd gone into my room to pack a few things. The girls came in and started bouncing on the bed. I played along. Neither Rebecca nor Hannah seemed to notice the wistful look in my eyes. For ten minutes we all played and laughed together, and I thought, *I hope this isn't the last time that I see my kids playing together, being children. I hope I get to see them grow up and experience life and that I'm with them when they do that.*

Then.

'Daddy needs to tell you something. Tomorrow I've got to go to a hospital and have an operation on my head to get rid of a nasty lump that is growing in there.'

'What do you mean?' cried Becky. 'What is wrong with you?' She burst into tears. Very reliant on me in all aspects of her life, Becky has quite openly said, 'If anything happens to you, Dad, I'll be following you.'

Hannah, who didn't fully understand the significance of what I'd said, reacted to Becky's tears. 'What's happened, Daddy?' she cried. 'What's wrong with Bec? Why is she crying?'

I calmed Rebecca down. 'I'm going to be okay. You know me. I'm strong. I'll get through it. I promise you nothing will happen. It is routine.'

I got up, went into the bathroom, buried my head in a towel and sobbed like a child for ten minutes. Pulling my head away from the towel, I looked at myself in the mirror. When I cry, my face turns into a map of red blotches, as if a rash has broken out. I stared in the mirror and said, 'Right, Watson. It is time to fucking pull yourself together.'

And that was it. That was the point where I accepted whatever the outcome of the operation would be.

* * *

In the morning I travelled to St George's Hospital in Tooting, south London. The night before the operation, I lay in my hospital bed feeling terrified that these would be my last few hours on earth. A member of the hospital staff walked in. I could see he was carrying something but, my eyesight being severely impaired, I couldn't make out what.

'Er, Meester Watson, I need you fill form for me.' He spoke with a thick Russian accent.

'I can't,' I said. 'I can't see. I can't even see a newspaper headline in front of my face.'

'Okay. I read out to you ... *Five per cent chance of death from blah blah, blah; 10 per cent chance of death from heart attack ... .15 per cent chance of complete blindness from XYZ ... .10 per cent chance of haemorrhage ...'*

He went through a laundry list of ghastly things that might happen to me.

'Are you okay to proceed with operation, Meester Watson?'

'Yes.'

'Please sign here.'

I applied the power squiggle.

'Thank you, Meester Watson. Good night.'

As he left the left the room, I called out to his back, 'Excuse me.'

'Yes, Meester Watson?'

'I never want to hear another bedtime story from you again.'

He laughed so much that I'm sure he nearly had bladder failure.

When my tumour and I were wheeled along to the operating theatre, the staff nurses and doctors lined the route. 'Good luck! Hope it goes well!'

I felt like Rocky Balboa making his way towards the ring. 'Dank you! Dank you v'much!'

When I arrived at the operating theatre, a nurse said, 'I'm going to give you an injection. Please count to ten.'

I made it as far as one.

The tumour was removed in the most common way of removing pituitary tumours: it involves – you may want to look away now – going up through the nose, cutting away the bone and delving into the skull. Henry Marsh, a pioneer surgeon who wrote the book on intercranial removal of tumours, led the operation.

When I came to, my first thought was, *I'm alive! Thank God!* But when I opened my eyes, all I saw was white opacity. If I placed my hand over my eyes, the white turned to dark grey.

Minutes later I heard a trolley rattle towards me, and a man's voice saying, 'Russell, my mum's a big fan. Would you be able to sign this for me?'

I thought: *Are you fucking serious? I've not even come out of recovery yet.*

'Yeah, yeah, what's her name?'

'Brenda. Thanks so much. She'll be over the moon.'

'No worries.'

Back home, my vision slowly began to clear, but it remained blurred and double, as if I was drunk or had water in my eyes. A clock face, for example, would appear as two images, one higher than the other, like the fragment of a kaleidoscope. My sight took four weeks to recover.

Still, I wasn't feeling right. Even six months after the operation, I felt tired and lethargic. If I shook my head, I kept thinking I could feel the tumour still there rattling around inside my skull. After the removal of a brain tumour, doctors may choose to put off radiotherapy.

There are two reasons for this. If the surgeon thinks they have removed all of the tumour, there is no need for radiotherapy. If the surgeon has left some tumour tissue behind, they may, because of the detrimental effects of radiotherapy, elect to wait and see if the residuum regrows or not. This is standard practice. No point in radiotherapy unless you absolutely need it.

8

'STAY WITH US, RUSSELL!'

IN 2007, WHILE still recovering, I began to record *Outside In*, my sixth and, as it turned out, final album with Decca. This album fell outside my original five-album deal. Decca wanted to sign me up to a new five-album deal, but I was wary. They were signing a host of new artists whom I felt they were prioritising. I agreed to a one-album deal, adding that if it went well we could do an extended deal.

I was playing football with my youngest, Hannah, in the garden and I went to kick a dead ball, swung a foot at it and missed . . . *Where the fuck is it?* I thought. I looked down. The ball was still there. I felt like a cold hand had gripped my heart. Everything in the universe turned on its side. *Please, not this again*, I thought.

I went for a brain scan.

'Mr Watson, we need to go back in,' said the doctor. 'There's another tumour.'

(My advice to anyone experiencing slight impairment

to their eyesight, especially in the peripheral vision, is: see a doctor.)

So many strange things happened around the time of my 'second' tumour. It was as if a higher force was shaping events and guiding me. Some coincidences seemed almost too coincidental to be coincidences. One moment stands out.

Window-shopping for brain surgeons, two caught my eye. 'Vinko Dolenc' is a name you don't forget. An internationally renowned, big-noise surgeon, Yugoslavia-born Dolenc is a famous exponent of surgery in the cavernous sinus area, true neurosurgical tiger country. The carotid artery, the major blood vessel that supplies the brain, and all the optical nerves either pass through, or near, this area. Dolenc and I spoke a few times by telephone. He told me how wonderful he was, ranked among the very finest surgeons for my type of tumour. He agreed to fly to London and meet me for a consultancy. Meanwhile, in my other ear, James Leggate, a consultant neurosurgeon in Manchester, whispered in professionally soothing tones: 'We can get this away for you, Russell, and you will return to where you should be.'

I got on well with Leggate. Well-spoken, he came across as intelligent, affable, cheerful, positive and with a good sense of humour. He was my kind of person, from the same reassuring mould as Bill Hayward and Patrick

McGuigan. At least, he seemed to get my jokes. Would he understand my tumour as well as he understood my sense of humour?

On the evening before I was due to meet Dolenc in London, Richard Thompson, my manager at the time from Merlin Elite, dropped by at my house. Standing six feet six, Richard is a smart, confident and slightly imposing figure. In every sense, he towers head and shoulders above the many managers who have worked for me over the years. A brilliant deal-originator, he packed a killer address book, and was deft at pulling strings, twisting arms and crunching toes. Whether fighting like a scrap-yard dog or tap-dancing on a razor's edge, he was good at getting deals over the line. When he later side-stepped farther into sports management, he put another bloke from Merlin Elite in charge of music. This other guy and I got along really well, but he just wasn't, well, Richard.

Over a take-away, Richard and I chewed over future projects, washed down with a glass or two.

'Richard, I don't feel too well, I'm going to hit the hay,' I said, 'in fact, I feel quite rough.' (It was around 10pm, early for me to go to bed).

Richard stayed overnight and left for London early the next morning. I was planning to leave later that day to meet Dolenc. Feeling more and more unwell and with faltering eyesight, I staggered up to bed. That evening I vomited profusely.

Normally I was up early, issuing instructions and generally annoying Victoria, my then assistant, and Gary, who also worked for me. That morning, however, I didn't show up. Gary rang. No answer. At eleven o'clock, Gary burst into my room and found me unconscious on the bed.

Not long afterwards, a team of paramedics, having managed to resuscitate me, had ripped my pyjamas off and were packing ice around my body. I was running a very high temperature of 42 degrees. The paramedics were worried I'd go into convulsions, which occur when your body temperature reaches a certain, very high, level. My temperature was well on the way to this point. I felt on fire. My head was in excruciating pain. My vision had shrunk to five per cent. I was semi-conscious. I had no control over my body. I couldn't move. All I could hear was one of the paramedics yelling, 'STAY WITH US, RUSSELL! KEEP YOUR EYES OPEN!'

The only words I managed to utter as the paramedics carried me downstairs to the ambulance were, 'Not too heavy for you, am I?' At least my sense of humour was intact.

One of the paramedics replied, 'We've carried 'em downstairs a lot heavier than you.'

During the drive to the hospital the atmosphere intensified. All I remember was one paramedic calling out to me, 'Stay with us Russell! . . . Russell, stay with us! . . . Don't close your eyes! . . . Don't go to sleep! . . . Stay with us Russell . . .' as if he was urging me to hang on to my life.

The surgeon on call that morning at the hospital happened to be James Leggate. I had been debating Dolenc vs Leggate for the previous weeks, and was still weighing up their respective merits when I went to bed the previous night. I never met Dolenc. Events tossed me into the hands of Leggate. Coincidence? God or fate preferring Leggate? I felt a sense of predestination, as if, not for the first time, I had been handed a script.

Of all the surgeons in all the hospitals, you had to come to this one.

Barely able to see while hearing doctors and nurses manoeuvring around me and talking to each other in raised and sometimes terse voices, I was wheeled into the MRI room and fed into the scanner. After the machine had been running for a couple of minutes, a weird feeling came over me. Everything seemed to stop. The pain in my head receded and the noise of the machine and the voices fell silent. Everything became black, peaceful, quiet and numb. Then a very strange thing happened. Out of the blackness emerged a vision of the door of the bedroom I slept in as a child when staying at my grandma's house. Fractionally ajar, it traced the outline of a sliver of light coming from the other side. I felt as though, if I reached out to open the door, I would be somehow be taking my leave and saying goodbye. *Okay,* I thought, *This is it. I'm ready for that. I'm ready to say goodbye and let go. Let go of everything.*

Then an image of my kids came into my head. I stopped myself, and said, 'No, I'm not ready! I'm not going! I'm not going to say goodbye. How will my children manage without me? They need me. I can't go yet.' I almost welcomed the return of the pain into my body. Then the vision dissolved, the emotions vanished and the real world came back – the clatter of the machine, the pain in my head, the constellations of lightbulbs above me, and the urgent, stressed voices of the medical staff. I was back in the MRI unit. I don't know what had happened to me, but it was the closest to death I have ever felt.

The tumour had haemorrhaged. Maybe it had been the pressure of being sick. The hospital dealt with the haemorrhage and pumped steroids into me.

As I lay in bed in the recovery room, Leggate came in. I was genuinely scared he was about to pass death sentence on me.

'The tumour on your pituitary has imploded and effectively died due to the haemorrhage,' said Leggate.

I exhaled deeply. At least I was still breathing.

'So what next?' I asked.

'Well, my advice is emergency surgery.'

I felt so frightened that I convinced myself I didn't want another operation. It seemed almost incredible that I was back in the same place I'd been just a year earlier. How could that possibly have happened? How would I get through another operation? If I survived, how would I endure the slow and painful recovery? And what if it happened again after that?

'I don't want another operation,' I said. 'I just want to go home and sit in my hot tub.'

'Why don't you want me to operate?' asked Leggate, forcing a good-natured smile.

'I got through my throat operation unscathed. I came through my first brain operation unscathed. I'm petrified that my luck has run out, that my nine lives are up. No one can be lucky enough to survive three operations.'

Leggate coughed gently, and then gave what sounded like a well-polished speech: 'I understand, Russell. But let me say this. There are many occasions when, in my line, I have to walk into this room, sit down, look the patient in the eye, and tell them there is nothing I can do.' Leggate held my gaze and looked at me intently. 'And let me tell you,' he continued, 'if there were just the nth of a chance of being able to do something for them, something that might save them, every one of these patients would grab it straight out of my hand, because that would be their only hope. But, although you may not think it now, you are one of the lucky ones. You have more than an nth of a chance. Much more. In your case, I think I can remove the tumour and that you will be okay. More than okay. You could make a full recovery. At the moment, we have everything under control. Think about it, Russell. When you have made your decision, there's a buzzer on the wall.'

Leggate got up and walked out of the room.

He never actually said, 'If I don't operate, you will die,' but that seemed to be the subtext of his speech. I was out of immediate danger, but, as I lay on the bed with thirty per cent vision, my trust in Leggate, helped along with a large dose of what felt like courage, overcame my fear of a further operation. I pressed the buzzer.

Leggate returned.

'Are we doing it?'

'Yes.'

'Wise decision, Russell. Good man.'

My second tumour was removed transsphenoidally by delving through the back of my top lip and entering the front of my skull. I still have the scar. Watch me carefully and you'll notice that the left-hand side of my lip doesn't move properly. If I open my mouth, the left-hand side will pretty much stay still, unless someone tells a really funny joke that cracks me up.

9

CAN YOU TASTE SALT?

IN GREAT PAIN, I came round from the anaesthetic to find concerned faces looking at me in the intensive care unit of the 'Alex', as the Alexandra Hospital is usually referred to. Rubber tubes and wires snaked from every orifice and limb.

'Can you taste salt, Mr Watson?' asked a nurse.

'Give me some and I'll tell you.'

'I mean, are you presently tasting salt?'

'No. Why? Does it matter?'

'It doesn't. Thank you, Mr Watson.'

The nurse then mumbled something to a colleague, who nodded and left the room.

I felt euphoric at being alive and relieved that I enjoyed full peripheral vision with none of the strange opacity that had clouded my sight after my first operation.

Euphoria was soon checked, however, at the thought

of having to oversee the mixing of *Outside In*, which I had been working on before I was hospitalised. For some reason this was all I could think about in those first days after I came round.

But I didn't want the album to come out. Not yet. I felt that it was wrong that it should be released while I was in and out of hospital. I wouldn't be able to promote it. Yet the incorrigible optimist in me took over. I began to think, *I really must get on with the job of helping put the album together.* A determination to do my best stole upon me. The 'passes' – a term that derives from the days when sound engineers kept track of how much tape had passed over the head stack to determine when cleaning and demagnetisation needed to be done, and which today refers to any recorded passage of music – had already been wrapped and Grant Ainsworth, my sound engineer, was ready to 'mix' the album, sifting for the best passes, sticking them together and striking a balance between different sounds.

Through the cat's cradle of wires and tubes, I fumbled for my phone.

'Grant, mate, come in and see me. Bring the passes with you. They want this album out by Christmas.'

Grant is one of life's characters and one of my favourite people. We'd met seven years earlier. Intelligent, knowledgeable, well-spoken and great company, he is a nineties child whose formative years were spent at the Hacienda, the legendary Manchester night club of the 1980s and early 1990s that New Order, the post-punk rock band, initially financed.

If you compare people's behavioural patterns to those of household pets, some people are like dogs: you pat them and feed them and they will stay loyal. Grant is like a cat: you can chuck him out of the back door at night and he will go off and do whatever he does and then come back when he is ready. We can meet for a drink after a gap of several months and pick up the conversation exactly where we left off. He's brilliant. If I ever need anything done in the realm of music, I can always rely on Grant. He is in every sense a 'sound' engineer.

'I can't do that, mate. No way.'

'Yes, you can. I'm not letting a record go out without hearing it first.'

'You're in intensive care, mate. Let it go.'

'I can't. It's my music. I need to listen to it, to make sure it is all correct.'

Producing an album is a complex process that wraps together artistry, technical wizardry, smoke, mirrors, hard work and a great deal of strange technical language. It can also involve sleepless night, tears, anguish, soul-searching, tantrums and, well, evidently stays in intensive care. It calls upon the talents, skills and resources of engineers who specialise in recording, sounding, mixing and mastering. So much can go right; so much more can go horribly wrong. I have been in studios and heard vocalists in the raw and thought, *Bloody hell, that's fantastic!* only for it to come back from the engineers sounding like fingernails on a blackboard.

When recording vocals in a studio, you never record one 'pass'. You have several goes. Take 'Nessun dorma'. I would record the first section . . .

Nessun dorma! Nessun dorma!

Tu pure, o Principessa

Nella Tua fredda stanza.

Stop.

I would record that section six times (some vocalists do as many as twenty takes), then go on to the next:

Guardi le stelle che tremano

D'amore e di speranza!

We record that six times. Then I do the next section, and so on until the aria is finished.

Then Grant will play me each pass, while I sift for gold.

' "Nessun dorma", take one. . . .'

'No!'

' "Nessun dorma", take two . . .'

'It's a bit flat.'

'Take three . . .'

'Urgh.'

'Take four . . .

'Ooh!'

'Take five . . .'

'Yes! Let's have a listen to that one again . . . I like that. Add take five to the mix.'

Or I might say to Grant, 'None of the passes of that last quarter section are lighting my candle. Let's do it again.'

So I would record the last section again, and again, if necessary.

That is how every recording artist works. I don't care what anyone says, no vocalist sings exactly as they sound on the finished album. There is always something done to improve the sound of their voice and the quality of the music.

This process is the perfect training ground and finishing school for anyone with a streak of perfectionism. I get involved in every step, forensically poring over every detail. If something goes unchecked, I can't sleep. It is my music. I want it to sound exactly as I want to hear it. I, and I alone, must decide which my best performance is, and I have to be sure that it appears in the finished album.

Not all artists are so hands-on. Many will turn up at

the studio with their recording engineer and sing a few passes. The recording engineer will say, 'Do another one for me . . . And another . . . One more . . . Lovely! There you go.'

The recording engineer will hand the recordings to the producer, who will retire with the sound engineer to mix them together. The artist, meanwhile, puts their feet up. The producer will send the finished album to the artist with a, 'Do you like this?'

'Er . . . Oh! . . . Yeah. Great.'

I am aware of some household names who even hire demo singers whose voices sound like their own, whom they use for the difficult notes. I know of other artists whose published voices can largely be credited to the Melodyne software which can pick out and tune individual sung notes, and can lengthen or shorten a vibrato. And I know of a few artists who are so shit at singing that their sound engineers have to work late into the night in order to render their voices bearable never mind commercial. More often than not, the artist themself is blissfully unaware.

'Oh my God, I sound amazing, don't I?'

'You do now.'

* * *

The next day, Grant arrived with the passes of the album on his iPod.

'Bloody hell, mate, what have they done to you?' A large plaster covered my nose, upper lip and the bottom half of my face. I looked like I was wearing a face mask. My eyes were blackened due to bruising. And my hair looked like a set-aside rewilding reserve. 'Does it hurt?'

'Course it bloody hurts. I also have someone playing the drums inside my head.'

'Did you know there is a traffic jam of news lorries outside?'

'No.'

'It looks like a go-slow at the Channel Tunnel crossed with a satellite tracking station. There are cables everywhere, and a load of film crews, reporters and paparazzi milling about waiting for news of your death.'

'Really?'

'Yeah. They are all asking, "Is he going to make it?", "Will Our Russ Die?"'

'You're kidding.'

'Seriously. You're all over the place mate.'

He thrust a newspaper at me. 'Russell Watson Fights for Life', screamed the headline.

'How the f . . .?'

To this day, I don't know how news leaked out, as I had hardly told anyone about my condition. Even close family members and friends only found out about it from the media. That is how quickly the networks were on to me.

'To business,' I said. 'Let's have a listen, then.'

I put on a pair of small headphones and pressed play.

'Strings are too high on this one . . . Cellos need to come up here . . . Vocal needs riding on this one a bit more . . . Not enough reverb on the voice . . . Push the level of the vocal up by one . . . piano needs to come down a bit in the mix . . .'

'I can't fucking believe I am doing this, mate,' said Grant as he sat on the end of my bed. 'This is outrageous. You're in intensive care.'

'We are doing it, so let's just crack on,' I said.

'If a nurse or doctor or anyone in a white coat walks in, I'm gonna get a serious bollocking.'

'We're just listening to music.'

'Mate, you've literally just been through a six-hour brain operation.'

Grant paid me two twenty-minute visits. On both occasions after listening to two or three songs, he'd say, 'I've got to go.'

'Just one more.'

'Mate! You are mental.'

I put down the iPod.

'Grant, there comes a point, soon reached in my case, as you well know, at which producing music stops being part of showbiz and becomes something altogether bigger. And I am willing to break visiting hour rules in order to achieve excellence. To love me and know me is to understand this. Okay?'

And that was how *Outside In* was put together.

To be fair to Grant, I knew that what I was doing was downright stupid. I had nearly died. We got the job done – but to what end? It were probably wiser had I put off the job until I was better. That would have meant the album would have been released after I had recovered and was able to promote it. Decca would have had no choice but to delay its release. Yet I still felt perversely and bizarrely compelled to get the job done. This represented the perfect illustration of my inability to let go, even in defiance of the most basic common sense, never mind hospital protocols.

* * *

After my stay in intensive care, tubes and pipes removed, most painfully the one attached to the end of my penis – Jeez, I can still feel it being extracted; made my eyes water – I was moved to a private room. Not having eaten properly for three days, I didn't need to do the other

121

stuff. Maybe they'd given me something. Very politely, and with an admirably straight face, a lady nurse told me, 'When you do go to the toilet, Russell, you've got to be very careful. This is because of what you've had done. When you need to go for a poo, it will be very difficult. Try not to strain. By the way, can you taste salt?'

She wasn't joking. Imagine a chunk of Yorkshire stone dropping out of your backside. I got a big – *ker-sploshh!* – splash on my arse.

The first thing that I wanted to know was when I could go home.

'I'll call the sister of the ward,' said a nurse.

A superior-looking lady entered and smiled professionally, head held high. 'How can we help you, Mr Watson?'

'When am I going to get out of here?'

'Good heavens!' she cried in a horrified falsetto. 'We don't get many patients who come straight out of intensive care and ask, "When can I go home?"' The ward sister began plumping pillows and adjusting bed clothes.

'I know, but when can I go home?'

'You can go home when you are ready to go home, Mr Watson.'

I felt a rising fit of irritation. 'This is a hospital, not a detention centre. I'm free to leave when I want, aren't I?'

'Yes, Mr Watson. You are free to leave whenever you choose.'

'Great, so I'll be off then; I'll be saying goodbye.'

The sister frowned at a clipboard that she had unhooked from the end of my bed.

'Mmm? The real question, Mr Watson, is whether you *can* leave, not whether you want to leave.' She looked at her watch.

I sensed a medical sermon coming on, a mix of technical lecture and church homily. 'What do you mean?' I asked.

'We must check that there aren't any infections, leakages or complications.'

'Leakages?'

'The brain is surrounded by a membrane that protects it from impact; it's like a sack. If it gets damaged, it leaks. We wouldn't want that, would we?'

'No,' I sighed heavily.

'Good. As I was saying, the shock to your system brought on by the operation means that your body may want time to rest, heal and recover. But please, Mr Watson, if you insist you're welcome to try to leave.'

'Right. Can you take this out?' A cannula was attached to my wrist.

'No.'

'Can you please just take it out?'

The ward sister gave a righteous martyr's sigh and removed the cannula.

I swung first one leg and then the other over the side of the creaking bed, then managed to raise my upper body so that I was sitting on the side of the bed. I pushed myself up and – *woah!* – fell straight back on to the bed. I felt dizzy and wiped out.

'Well, Mr Watson, let's try something more manageable, shall we? Outside your room, there is a long corridor. At the end of the corridor, there is a flight of stairs going up. Let's say that the day you can walk along the corridor and then up the flight of stairs and back is the day that you can go home. Mmm?' End of sermon.

The sister left the room. A couple of seconds later, she reappeared. 'Can you taste salt?'

For the next two weeks, the corridor outside my room became the sole focus of my life and being. At first I walked at a snail's pace. With each day, I gained speed, confidence and distance. I had corridor vision. Crisp, white-coated nurses with neat hair click-clacked past and gave me encouragement.

'Well done, Mr Watson.'

'Thanks,' I said, with just a hint of irony.

'That's the spirit, Mr Watson. With our backs to the wall . . .'

'Yeah, we put our best foot forward. Thank you.'

Meanwhile, my room filled with balloons, presents, messages and enough flowers for a Mob funeral. This one was from Mary from Bolton, that one was from Jean and Bill from Oldham, the one over there was from Anne in Wigan. I appreciated them all.

Among the cards was one from Diane Sawyer, the US television anchor: 'Sorry to hear about your plight.' In the early noughties, *Good Morning America*, the news programme broadcast from New York City, had invited me on to the show as often as *Loose Women* had in the UK. The producers seemed to take a shine to me. I became a 'friend of the show'.

On one occasion, Diane Sawyer was the presenter. There are moments when people say things that stick in the mind but whose real significance dawns on you only years later. When I saw her card as I lay in the recovery room at the Alex, my mind replayed her brief speech introducing me to the programme: 'He sings like Pavarotti and he talks like he's one of the Beatles.' I remember thinking at the time that she was just another presenter of a television show. As it turned out, she was *the* Diane Sawyer! To be fair, she probably thought I was just another singer with a good voice.

A couple of guys from Decca travelled up from London to see me, which was kind of them. It is well known in the record industry that, when a star dies, their sales rocket. I wonder if it crossed anyone's mind to check the warehouse stock of my back catalogue.

After eleven days, I was the hero of eleven sorties along the hospital corridor and back. On the twelfth, I made it to the far end. I buzzed the ward sister. 'I've got to the end of the corridor. I'll be up the stairs tomorrow. Can I go home?'

'Home?' She made 'home' sound it was like a place only a lunatic would want to go.

'Yes. Home.'

'Mr Watson, why are you so desperate to get out of here? We are looking after you. This is the best place for you.'

'It is my daughter Rebecca's thirteenth birthday on 31 October. I want to be out of here for that.'

I wasn't thinking about getting back on stage and singing. All I was thinking about was getting out for my daughter's birthday. That was my focus. And I did. I discharged myself on the afternoon of 31 October.

Back home, despite it being early winter, I marvelled at the brilliant colours of flowers and plants in my garden.

In a follow-up consultancy, I told Leggate, 'I cannot believe my sight. I can see everything and in colour too. Everything seems so vivid, clean and crisp. It is as if I have new eyes.'

'That's how it should be. We've got rid of the tumour and relieved the pressure on the optic nerve.'

All was not over however, as I was about to face a complicated course of radiotherapy. Oh – and thankfully I did not ever taste salt . . .

10

IT ISN'T OVER UNTIL
THE FAT MAN SINGS

RELEASED TWO DAYS after my forty-first birthday, *Outside In* flat-lined. I was in no state to promote the album. In show business, the show must always go on, even if the star is stuck somewhere between intensive care and the radiotherapy unit. Decca probably reckoned that my fame would do the work of promoting it and that the album would sell itself on the principal that the public always flocks to the scene of a disaster.

He's just had a brain tumour. Let's have a listen.

The album contains the lovely 'La Califfa' by Ennio Morricone, a song that filled a million hearts. Otherwise, if you are a forgetful person, this is the album for you. There are plenty of tracks to forget.

Notwithstanding Grant and my defiance of white-coat protocols, it was an album where a survival mechanism switched on. I'd been used to massive success, huge sales and big numbers. When an album falls short, defensive measures are needed in order to preserve sanity. If an album flops or if its production or promotion is compromised, I will redact it from my mind. As a performing artist, especially as a vocalist, confidence is king, emperor and Pope. Anything that risks puncturing or undermining confidence must be expunged. If an album does less well than I expected it to, and I am asked, 'How did it do?', I would never say, 'It bombed. It was a pile of shit. The record company hated it and no one bought it.' I would spin it as, 'Yeah, it did okay. It didn't quite meet expectations, but the market is tough.'

The music industry operates in an even more brutal way. An album that flops on week one won't see week two. Neither artist nor label will ever discuss it again. The music industry doesn't do flash-to-bang times. Everything has to be now-now-now instantaneous, otherwise you fail. The phone falls silent until your next release is being planned. You have to sustain a level of output, performance, quality and consistency to keep the cash tills ringing or you die.

In show business, you cannot plug numbers into a model and solve the future. You cannot know where you end up until you take the journey. It's impossible. Of course, you need to be aware of the gaps between where you are, where you think you are, where you need to be, and where you want to be. Trying to concertina those gaps together so that they disappear, and your dreams and reality coincide and become one, is part of the thrill of showbiz and one of my main motivations. In order to have the necessary drive to achieve this, you need a strong, 3-D, full-colour vision of what you are aiming for. This vision also has the psychological benefit of distracting you from the terrifying cliff face of failure.

*   *   *

So I tried to tune out of the sound of silence around the new album's release. Harder to ignore was the prospect of twenty-five doses of radiotherapy, beginning on 2 January 2008 at the Christie Hospital in Manchester. The post-op euphoria at being alive, sighted and seeing my daughters was quickly tempered. While I was nervous about the prospect of the radiotherapy itself, I was also fast developing fears and phobias about the medical establishment, hang-ups that would inspire some, shall we say, imaginative coping strategies. I realise, however, that the prognosis could have been far worse. Had the tumour been cancerous the outlook would have been very grim.

Radiotherapy kills cells. It is particularly effective at killing tumour cells, which turn over more rapidly than healthy cells, so are more susceptible to injury, in the same way that you are more likely to get food poisoning if you eat a lot of something that is bad for you, rather than a little.

Radiotherapy has a role in treating pituitary tumours where the surgeon cannot physically remove every bit of tumour because of the volatile area that it inhabits. If there is a residuum, the doctors usually wait and see if it regrows. If it regrows and the surgeon throws up their hands and says, 'I can do no more,' radiotherapy comes into play. Alternatively, the doctors can decide to irradiate immediately, which is what they did with me.

One of the downsides of radiotherapy is exhaustion. While it is designed to maximise injury to the tumour cells, the healthy bits of your brain dislike it. Brain injuries can result in specific conditions like paralysis, but there are other more subtle but common reactions to radiotherapy such as headaches and lethargy, in exactly the same way that concussion causes fatigue. The exhaustion from radiotherapy usually lasts a few months.

When I turned up for the first blast of radiotherapy – 'Happy New Year, Mr Watson!' – I was told to put on the tailor-made mask and mouth shield that I had previously had fitted, and lie down on what looked like a meat slab to be bolted to a mainframe, so that I couldn't move. If I so much as twitched, a nurse would say, 'Don't move your face or eyebrows, Mr Watson. Keep completely still for a few seconds while we fire the radiation.'

The operation and the treatment caused swelling, for which I was prescribed steroids, and given a list of potential side effects, most of which I ignored.

My consultant endocrinologist gravely warned me in his soft Scottish accent, 'Do you realise that you will never be as you were before? The concoction of medication you are taking will have a big impact. You're going to be taking Genotropin, which is a growth hormone, as well as testosterone and hydrocortisone. These will affect your day-to-day life, so things will not be so easy . . .'

Presumably he thought that he was being open and realistic about what firing radiation into the pituitary does to you. His bedside manner grated. His attitude crossed all my red lines about positivity. If someone tells me, 'You can't do this' or 'You'll never be able to achieve that', all I hear is the starting gun in a race to go out and accomplish exactly what I've been told is beyond me. Twice. And take a photo. My wife Louise says that my refusal to be beaten is the reason I'm still alive.

'I don't need a synopsis of what I can and can't do for the rest of my life,' I snapped. 'Tell me what I need to know, and I'll clear off.'

* * *

It is easy to get bogged down with personal struggles and day-to-day stuff. It is easier to moan about them than find solutions. When I came away from my first and second brain operations, I was determined that I wouldn't play the victim and that I wasn't going to sit around and let the after-effects consume me. Systematically, I was going to fight my way to recovery. But I knew it would be slow and a process, not instantaneous. When I emerged from my second brain operation, people asked if I was worried whether I would sing again. I thought, *Bollocks, I'm not worried about whether I'll sing again. I'm worried about whether I'll breathe again.* Nor was I thinking about singing when I lay on the meat slab having radiation blasted into my skull. All I was thinking was that I must take my recovery one step at a time: have the operation; survive the operation; submit to five sessions of radiotherapy a week for five weeks; recover fitness; and so on.

Just before I completed my course of radiotherapy in early February 2008, I was walking downstairs at home one morning when, just as I descended to the hallway, I unexpectedly saw a nineteen-stone chipmunk, with hair falling out in clumps, coming towards me. His shorts and T-shirt were striving to do difficult jobs.

'Oh my God!' I said to the chipmunk. 'Are you me? You don't look like me.'

Every ounce of the person I once was had vanished. All that remained was a nineteen-stone rodent. Not only my appearance, weight and bulk, it was also the person inside who seemed to have undergone a hideous transformation. Neither superstar nor performer nor even Russell Watson, I was just a list of symptoms in shorts and T-shirt. I was so depressed about this afterwards that I turned the mirror round to face the wall, so that I wouldn't catch sight of my reflection any more.

'Jesus Christ!' I said to myself. 'Must be the steroids!'

A side-effect of steroids is feeling bloody starving all the time. Every morning, after a full English, I would graze my way towards lunch, which would be a sandwich, a packet of biscuits and a can of Coke. After more grazing, dinner would be another packet of biscuits and some sort of ready-meal. I couldn't stop. I was chunking it on. I looked like I'd eaten a bigger version of myself. I'd erupted, bulged and ballooned. Confronting the nineteen-stone squirrel, I began desperately looking for forensic evidence of the artist formerly known as Russell Watson.

More than the prospect of imminent death or the machinations of record labels or my attempted character assassination by critics or even the sight of the dreaded giant chipmunk, the only things that really upset me are the loss of family members, friends and pets whom I have loved, and what my daughters had to endure while I was at death's door. Everything else, I accept. Well . . .

When young, I likened my dad to an Ancient Greek hero to whom I gave mythical qualities. My daughters thought the same of me. I was the Watsonator, the Salford Atlas, an invincible force of nature with the voice of ten men that could shake foundations. Yet here was this tragic, pathetic figure. After two serious operations and a course of radiotherapy, my steroid-pumped body had become a human dirigible. I always used to play with Rebecca and Hannah in the garden, go on walks with them, take them shopping. A few months later, I wasn't a tenth of that dad. I had no energy.

In retrospect, while this was horribly upsetting for my daughters, there is actually nothing healthier for a thir-teen-year-old girl than to discover that her father turns out not to be Superman, but in fact a loving bloke with frailties, faults and flaws. Peddling myths that pretend otherwise is probably unwise.

I rolled out of radiotherapy feeling obliterated. In an unnerving flashback to a long-dead six-year career on the shop floor in Salford cutting bolts and assembling crank-shafts, I wondered if my time in the strobe of fame was over. I had gone from summit to plummet. What then? A handful of loyalists who had made my life a glittering cavalcade of sparkling engagements and peeled blueberries had charitably stuck around. My assistant Victoria, who was always at the centre of much chaos and hilarity, showed up five days a week. Every day, Gary had driven me in a rather spectacular car the forty-five minutes to the Christie hospital for my radiotherapy sessions. As we drove, I remember thinking, *I'm so bloody lucky to have Victoria and Gary around me. A lot of people are going through the same shit as me, but they have to find their own way to and from the hospital.* As much as it was a nightmare for me, I felt fortunate and grateful that I could rely on the support mechanism that Victoria and Gary provided. I was particularly grateful to Gary that he had found me when my tumour haemorrhaged.

* * *

Sticking to my step-by-step recovery plan, I needed to shed the excess kilos, deflate the giant chipmunk dirigible, and get fit. I called 'Red' Steve Gallagher, an old friend and a proper Salford lad. He is known as Red Steve not because he is a Manchester United fan, but because he is, well, red. He always has a red face. In the sun, his face becomes incandescent.

'Steve, I need to get out of the house and get fit. Can you help?'

Steve dropped by soon afterwards. 'All right, our kid,' he said. 'Maybe we can go for a walk down the road or something like that. You don't want to go in too heavy. You've been through a lot in recent months.'

'Yeah, okay. Let's go.'

Within five minutes of leaving the house, I was sweating profusely and feeling exhausted. Red Steve looked at me. 'I think we should go back, our kid.'

Every day, Red Steve and I stepped out of the front door and went for a walk. Five minutes became five-and-a-half minutes became six minutes became seven and so on up to half an hour. Before I knew it, I was walking without sweating or feeling exhausted.

Right, I thought, *now I need to get properly fit.*

Victoria rang my local Total Fitness gym. 'Russell Watson wants to join. He'll be coming in on Monday. He'd like a coach to help ease him back to fitness.'

Arriving at the gym, I found the manager waiting for me at the door. He had a wheelchair with him. I laughed.

'I'm okay,' I said. 'I don't need the wheelchair just yet.'

I was put in the care of Glen, a personal trainer.

Two flights of stairs rose to the gym. I made it up the first, but when I summited the second I was out of breath and panting hard.

'All right, Russell,' said Glen. 'Looks like we've got a lot of work to do, pal.'

Had I simultaneously attempted an almighty, holistic, marathon restoration of my entire person in all aspects of well-being, including the physical and psychological, I doubt I'd have made it. By separating my recovery into discrete phases, I could progress.

*   *   *

Radiotherapy administered the last rites to my pituitary gland, the body's equivalent of the CPU in a computer, the ingenious circuitry that interprets, processes and executes instructions from hardware and software platforms. Responsible for secreting hormones, a healthy pituitary releases cortisone, a steroid hormone that flows into the bloodstream whenever you are stressed. It generates testosterone, the male hormone; and it produces growth hormone. Without a functioning pituitary, I have to inject, ingest or apply all these hormones every day, in order to make myself a functioning human being.

Ordinarily, when you wake up in the morning your brain automatically sends the pituitary a message, which in turn sends a message to the adrenal gland, which secretes cortisone into the bloodstream, which converts it to cortisol. This complex process is how you wake up in the morning.

If you get a lull in the afternoon, your body sends another message down the daisy chain to fire you up again.

When I wake up, none of that happens. I usually feel like I'm going down with flu. The first thing I do is take hydrocortisone. At first, in order to get 20mg of hydrocortisone into my system, I would have to take 10mg in the morning, 5mg at lunch and 10mg at night. If I forgot any of those doses, red blotches would appear on my skin and I'd become vague and stop making sense, assuming I made any in the first place. Hydrocortisone keeps me alive; three or four days without it would kill me. I cannot function without it. Now, thanks to breakthroughs in hormone replacement medication, I can take one tablet that lasts all day.

Human vanity being what it is, it is easy to assume that your personality is largely the product of all your life experiences as interpreted by a mysterious and unique series of combustions in the brain. Well, I'm sorry to disappoint you. Much of what we call 'personality' is down to hormones. If I produce too much testosterone, I get angry. If I don't take enough growth hormone – or Genotropin in its laboratory-made formulation – I feel introverted and antisocial: the phone rings; I can't be bothered to pick up. With normal levels of growth hormone, I'd be, 'Hello! How are you?'

Living on hormone replacements and steroids is a challenge in itself. It's a balancing act in a howling gale. The identical dose of a particular hormone may have a different effect from one day to the next. It goes beyond simply throwing back the meds and cracking on. My waking-up routine takes me about one hour. If I still feel dreadful, I'll ring Dr Tara Kearney, consultant endocrinologist at the Alexandra Hospital in Manchester. Tara is the Oracle and confidante of the endocrine system, and my long-suffering guardian angel.

'Tara, it has taken me two hours to wake up, and I still feel . . .'

'You need to adjust your steroids, Russell. You need to increase X and decrease Y.'

Tara is medically to me what Grant Ainsworth is musically. She helps me get the mix right and strike the balance. She understands what I've been through. She has been a constant in my life of extreme ups and downs.

After much determined experimentation, I have got the hang of balancing the hormones so that all parts take equal strain, to borrow a naval expression, and I can start to create the album of my human self. I have distilled the fine art of hormone replacement down to a daily routine akin to brushing my teeth only much more time-consuming.

The abundant pharmacopoeia that I carry often attracts attention. Travelling abroad, I pack syringes and all kinds of medication in a proper medic's bag.

'Are you a doctor?' asks the flight attendant as I board the aeroplane.

'No, but with my knowledge of everything I've had wrong with me, I might as well be.'

However much I prepare before I travel – and these days I must be really organised – problems can arise, especially if I get sick when travelling and I can't keep down oral medication. Normally, if anyone who is on the drugs that I'm on gets sick, they would have to go to hospital and be put on a drip.

In February 2013, I was invited to sing 'The Prayer' at the launch of a BMW 7 series car in China. The organisers flew Natasha Marsh – a soprano who usually sings with me when I do engagements overseas – my management team, Gary, my assistant and me first class, and put us up in a beautiful hotel. On the evening before the launch, BMW kindly hosted us at a traditional Chinese banquet. The food turned out not to agree with us. As soon as I returned to my hotel room, I began to feel unwell and was sick all night. Natasha was suffering the same fate.

My hydrocortisone, which I take daily, is an oral drug. Normally when I am unwell, I must double my intake, such as on occasions like this when nothing is staying down. In the morning, I therefore rang Tara to ask her advice and explained I couldn't keep anything down.

'You have to inject the steroids intra-muscularly,' she said. 'You're going to have to stab yourself with a needle in the quadriceps muscle. That's the one at the front of your thigh. You'll have to use the three-inch needle. Just push it in.'

Fuck, I thought, when I produced this three-inch needle from my medicine chest. *I am used to injecting myself every day, but with a much smaller pin. This looks like the mother of all needles. What if I hit the bone?*

'What do you mean "Just push it in"?' I asked.

'You've got to push the needle straight in and, once in, don't move your leg, okay?'

Gritting my teeth and holding my breath, I literally went *bumpf* – and plunged the needle into my leg.

'Ah-ah-ah-ah!'

'Don't move your leg!'

The serum inside the hydrocortisone is quite viscous. As you push it in, the muscles resist it. The harder you depress the plunger, the greater the resistance and the pain. I probably looked like a character in one of those war movies where the injured soldier has to stab himself with a syringe to stay alive. Well, that's how I felt.

'Now you have to inject metoclopramide, the anti-sickness drug.'

'Oh for f . . .!'

My manager rang in the morning to check if everything was okay.

'No,' I said, 'I'm as sick as a dog. I've been vomiting all night. My throat is shredded from heaving. It's sheer driving hell.'

Natasha similarly had been up all night and could barely speak.

One of the worst things that can happen to a singer is vomiting. When the contents of your stomach come up and there is nothing left, you bring up bile, an acid that burns the larynx.

'I can't sing,' I said. 'I'm still sick.'

A few minutes later, the lady from BMW who had organised the launch came on the phone. 'You have to sing,' she said.

'I can't,' I said, kneeling on the floor of the bathroom. 'You need to talk to my assistant.'

I handed Gary the phone. 'Mr Watson is unable to sing. He's sick. Ms Marsh is likewise indisposed.'

The organiser wasn't having this. She pushed hard. 'The whole event is reliant on you. You need to perform. You need to perform.'

She would not accept 'no' for an answer.

The organisers came up with a cunning plan. I'd recorded 'The Prayer' with Lulu on *Encore*, my second album. The plan was that Natasha and I would lip-synch to a backtrack of 'The Prayer' lifted from *Encore*.

Lip-synch.

The very word sends a shiver down my spine. The greatest insult you can hurl at a singer is to accuse him or her of lip-synching.

Natasha and I discussed this idea in between bouts of vomiting and encounters with three-inch needles. It was far from ideal, but we agreed it was the only viable solution.

Natasha was nervous. I told her that, in order to conceal any fractional delay in the synchrony between music and lip movement, you have to make love to the microphone, holding it tight to your mouth and cupping it with your hands.

'Don't create any room for ambiguity,' I said. 'Push your mouth against the microphone and that'll do it.'

White as ghosts, sick bags in hand, we made it to the mini-stadium where the launch was being held.

In the performance, despite still feeling rough, I struggled to keep a straight face. I found it funny to see Natasha, a professional, classically trained soprano, miming to Lulu, whose gravelly, pop-y timbre sounds nothing like hers.

145

BMW executives and their guests leapt to their feet clapping. I turned to Natasha. 'It may not have been art but we suffered for it.' Afterwards Natasha tweeted, 'Never eating tuna again!'

Aside from the day-to-day practicalities that come with relying on medication, I have learnt a whole new psychology and a different kind of physiology. I have discovered that my brain works more strangely than I had imagined, predominantly based on the output of hormones into my body and how they affect me. I have a gel that I use for testosterone. When I first wake in the morning I rub it on to either my stomach or inner thighs. I have become acutely aware of where my testosterone levels sit, be they high, low or just right. When it's low I get what I can only describe as a foggy head. My concentration levels dip and I start to feel overly emotional. The slightest thing can often bring floods of tears for no apparent reason. If it's high then the polar opposite occurs. I get a sense that I can take on the world, I feel dispassionate and my tolerance levels disappear. When it's at a normal level – well, in plain and simple terms, I feel normal. This is the most preferable state to be in . . .

At least now I have a better idea of what's going on with me. But something else puzzled me. Around 2008, a strange introversion came over me. I felt anti-social and didn't want to see anyone, do anything or leave the house. Other than to perform, leaving the house became an ordeal. When I readied myself for a night out, my neck would redden. I'd feel hot, tired and stressed. The sight of food brought out a sweat. Uncomfortable and unconfident, I wanted neither to see nor be seen. It might have been the tumour causing havoc with my pituitary, or it could have been a confidence thing due to the effect of steroids and the stress of getting back on my feet after my financial problems. I resented what I saw as the hypocrisy and superficiality of the comfort and company of society. The guy who as a kid was often the team leader, who in later years was the life and soul, who seized every opportunity and who crashed Bill Clinton's fundraiser, seemed to have taken leave of absence. Even years after my second brain operation, this strange in-growing personality and low-grade depression persisted. Friends assumed I was suffering the after-effects of two serious illnesses. Perhaps I was.

Thankfully, this inwardness never seemed to apply when I was performing. As soon as the warmth of the spotlight flooded my face, the adrenaline would flow. I've always been like that. Once I woke up at 3 in the morning. I was thirsty, so I went downstairs for a glass of milk. I opened the fridge door, the light hit my face and I ended up doing a twenty-minute spot there and then. My adrenal gland at least seems to have been unaffected by pituitary loss.

The problem is that hormones only get you so far. They are not a sovereign panacea to mood adjustment and emotional stability. If I'm feeling low, and the drugs don't seem to work, or if I can't strike a balance and Tara has gone offline, I will sit down and say, 'Right, I've gotta fight this. I'll have a swim and then I'll feel all right.' But I have to get things going myself. I can't just sit back and say, 'I give up. Come and get me.' In order to perform, go on tour, socialise and be a normal human being following pituitary apoplexy, I need the same determination that got me from working night shifts in a factory to becoming Britain's bestselling classical vocalist.

11

BACK ON TOUR

A FEW MONTHS after radiation therapy ended, exhausted and downbeat, I began to try out my voice at home when there was no one around. It was an experiment that yielded depressing results. My voice continued to function but with increasing pathos. Some of the upper register was no longer there. I would tire easily. I couldn't figure out why. There was no clear-cut answer. Were the hormones thickening my vocal folds? Was I taking too much testosterone? Had the removal of the tumour altered the acoustics of my head and vocal folds? I scaled back my repertoire.

When I eventually climbed back on to a stage, one piece stood out. It was the Bach/Gounod 'Ave Maria' that Charles Gounod, the French Romantic composer, created by superimposing a melody of his own creation on to J. S. Bach's famous Prelude No 1 in C Major from Book One of *The Well-Tempered Clavier* and turning it into a prayer.

The joy of being back on stage was almost overwhelming. Even though I'd taken it down a semitone so that the highest note was A flat, the emotion of singing that aria was ten times greater than normal.

Whereas in the past, working with Bill and then Patrick McGuigan, or just by myself, I had pushed myself, challenged myself to improve and fine-tune my voice, now I adopted a conservative approach and stuck to the golden rule of performing vocalists: stay within your singing range. Getting back on tour, I sang nothing stronger than one or two pieces that Mario Lanza popularised up to F sharp, or on a good day G. I wouldn't touch the great classical arias, 'Vesti la giubba' or 'E lucevan le stelle', nor 'Caruso'. Despite our long and significant relationship, I couldn't even consider 'Nessun dorma'. I didn't think I'd be bringing anyone to their feet with that final high B. *Vincerò?* Unlikely. I was getting by on a middle-of-the-road diet of musical theatre numbers, like 'Sixteen Tons' and 'What a Wonderful World'. To my relief, the public was still buying it. Or were they?

As part of my conservative approach, I dropped 'O sole mio', my whizz-bang, sure-fire, crowd-warming overture, by a semi-tone to end on A flat. I got a good response. And yet. And yet ... Most audience members won't know when I have dropped a key. Unless they have perfect pitch, they won't be sitting there thinking, *Well, this is slightly lower.* However, they can still *tell.* With the human body's exquisite powers of discrimination, on some fundamental level audiences know. Proper key: *ClapClapClapClap.* Semitone lower: *clap-clap-clap.* They don't know they know, or how they know, but they just do. They may not go in search of it, nor always fully appreciate it when they find it, but everyone still loves quality and authenticity.

* * *

In thirty-five years of singing to live audiences up and down the land, I've noticed one or two slight but definable regional variations – Oxford audiences tend to be more reserved than, say, Glaswegian audiences – but external factors tend to take priority. What is on the news? What is being fed to the audience? Doom and gloom? What about the weather? If it has been pouring down for two weeks and I have a gig on a Tuesday night in Newcastle in the freezing cold and the news is misery, I will not get the same response as on a Saturday night when the sun is shining, the audience has had a few beers, and England have beaten Germany at football. Sometimes it is a time/place thing. Saturday night in Liverpool feels very different to Monday night in London.

The toughest crowd, the most demanding focus group

in show business, is your home crowd on home turf. They've seen you perform umpteen times. You want to put on a good show. Friends and family might show up. You feel the pressure. Every time I perform in Manchester, I have to pull something new out of the bag, otherwise they go, 'He did all this last time we came to see 'im.'

Whether a club near my home, or 73,000 people in a stadium, I'm good at getting an audience onside. That represents a skill in itself. My father always said I was 'gifted with the gramophone needle. If England had a team of talkers, you would be captain, Russ.'

In my early career, if I thought the audience was engaged and interested, I'd be with them all the way. If not, I'd flip into 'club mode', which is one up from phoning it in. In my head, I'd be saying to them, 'If you are going to smoke, drink, sit and chat all night, fair enough. I'll sing my songs, pick up my £70 and go home.'

At one gig in Wigan during my pubs-and-clubs phase, I was picking up zero interest, not even a tingle. At half-time, I came off feeling dejected. The concert secretary came up to me.

'You all right, lad?'

'Yes, not too bad.'

'Hard work in here. You'll never get them on yer side, lad, but you are doing a good job.'

I thought, *Never get them onside? I'll show you.* I went

out and I worked the room with every ounce of my being. I took the audience by the scruff of the neck, metaphorically speaking, and gave them everything I had. I left it all on the stage. And they loved it.

He's brilliant! Best artist we'd had on this year! Get him in for Christmas Eve!

I left Wigan thinking, *I am never switching to autopilot again. I am never coasting, never sitting back.* And I never have. If I do a gig and the audience is not responding, I will do whatever I can to get them onside. If there is one person listening to me or 100,000 or just my long-suffering dog, it still matters. Even if I'm on my own, it matters.

Ten years in the clubs taught me a few tricks. I can pretty much deal with most eventualities, from equipment failure to some serious heckling. When performing, I adjust my onstage manner according to what sort of audience I think I have. I'll try a few jokes or wry asides, but if I get no bounce-back I go into what I call 'Serious Classical Mode'. If that's what the audience wants, I'll keep everything formal and go with the flow.

A good way of finding out what kind of audience I have is to ask, 'Who knows what the world's most successful musical of all time is?'

Normally, I get the response, '*Phantom of the Opera*' or '*Les Misérables*'.

When I posed this question at a concert in Yorkshire,

153

a chap bounced up from his chair eight rows from the front.

'*Grrrrrease!*' he shouted, at the top of his voice.

'No, sir, it's not *Grease*.'

'Yes, it is.'

'No, it's not.'

'Yes, it is, Russell. It's *Grease*. One hundred per cent I know it's *Grease* and I'm not having it any other way, pal. You can go and check with Google on your phone. It's *Grease*.'

'Okay then,' I conceded, after a few more volleys of hoarse Yorkshire words had flown in from the stalls. 'We are going to sing something now from the world's *second* most successful musical, which of course is *Les Misérables*.'

Sometimes the audience lets you know what they think without you asking. At a concert at the Brighton Dome, a woman began shouting stuff from the balcony and carried on well into the programme. It was hilarious for me, but I'm sure it was more than distracting for the audience. Engage or ignore? Eventually, I paused the programme and called back, 'What are you shouting? I can't understand you.'

'Get on with it!' she bawled.

'Well, I'm not going to respond to that, am I? Why don't you get on with it and go home.'

'I bloody will then.'

She got up and walked out.

'Thank you,' I said, and carried on. Thirty seconds later, an almighty bang resonated throughout the auditorium.

'Somewhere in the distance,' I quickly quipped, 'a door slammed.' The audience cracked up.

On another occasion, a bloke in the audience was shouting out in between each song.

'*Blah, blah, blah* . . . Can you not sing "Nessun dorma"? I rather like that one . . . *blah, blah, blah.*'

So I stopped the programme and said to him, 'Do you want to come on stage and do a five-minute spot while I go backstage, put my feet up and have a glass of wine or something?'

'No. Shut up!'

Instances like this don't bother me. Usually, I smile and carry on. Ideally, I will walk on stage and win the audience over with a decent performance. Afterwards, the audience will wander home dazed and slightly bewildered, in a state of pleasurable shock but feeling at peace with the world, while I go home thinking how lucky I am to have this wonderful job. Ordinarily, I am confident enough not to let audience 'participation' put me off. Or so I thought, until a singular, seemingly innocuous moment one evening that turned my life on its head.

In spring 2009, I launched into my first large-scale UK tour since my second brain operation. I was backed by Liverpool's Sense of Sound Singers, who had caught my ear on *Last Choir Standing*. We were selling out big theatres like Birmingham Symphony Hall, which seats 2,500, and doing consecutive nights at the Lowry in Manchester, which holds 1,730. I put on a series of concerts that year as part of a huge UK tour. I couldn't help wondering how many of the audience were turning up just to check I was still alive. This was the Morbid Curiosity Comeback tour.

Wary of not being able to hit the high notes of my usual classical operatic repertoire, I adjusted my programme downwards to make an easier sing of it. Instead of opening with my usual 'O sole mio', I began with 'Somewhere' from *West Side Story* followed by 'Panis angelicus', a beautiful piece that floods the soul but is not one that strikes fear into the hearts of tenors. It is a stop-gap, almost a rest. Then came a Sinatra-style version of 'Strangers in the Night'; a run-out for a tenor and a million miles from tough arias like 'Vesti la giubba', 'Funiculì, funiculà' or 'Caruso'. No singer can belt out high-octane pieces like 'Nessun dorma' all evening, not even Pavarotti, but this programme came nowhere near close to being what I would ordinarily consider challenging.

At one concert, I had finished singing 'Strangers in the

Night'. As the polite applause died down, I said, 'Thank you very much.' I never look the audience in the eye, nor pick out individual members. I may occasionally allow myself a glance. If I see a familiar face, I might nod. Comedians might make eye contact; musicians and singers rarely do. Besides, the bright lights mean that I can only see the first few rows. On this occasion, bang in front of me, three rows in, sat a couple who had already snagged my attention by chatting in between pieces. Audiences don't normally talk at my gigs; they watch and listen in silent self-communion. This bloke, however, leaned over to his wife and said audibly, 'He's not what he used to be, is he love? Wake me up when it's over.'

Every word hit me like a freight train.

Okay, I thought, *stay calm.*

A complex matrix of thoughts flashed through my mind. I'd held the zeitgeist in my hand and savoured the incomparable taste of fame as I packed out stadia and auditoria and hit number one; now, I was reduced to a Russell Watson tribute act, treading water, ticking boxes, singing spreadable, low-cal, middle-of-the-road stuff.

I had no need to resist the temptation to put the mic down and explain to the bloke, in words that reflected my feelings, all that I'd been through over the past eight years. I knew he was right. I was taking the line of least resistance to keep things going. I'd gone from great to yawn, a washed-up, frustrated, side-lined has-been. Was I simply whistling in the dark? Was I singing to drown out the voices in my head screaming, 'You're finished!' It took this bloke in row three to make me face this reality and spur me into taking action. Whoever you are, thank you. If we met, I'd shake your hand. I now see that part of me was thinking, *No one will notice; I can get away with singing 'Music of the Night' from* Phantom of the Opera *instead of 'Nessun dorma' or 'Caruso' or 'Ave Maria' or 'O sole mio'.* Well, they did notice, and I couldn't. People seemed pleased to turn up and watch me sing, but they knew – and now I knew that they knew – that I'd only clawed my way back to 'not as good as he used to be'.

Come on, Russell, you're better than this!

The nineteen-stone chipmunk encounter was a catalyst that helped me get a grip, but that grip wasn't enough. 'He's not what he used to be' was not so much a catalyst as a detonator and well worth a needlepoint cushion.

People who know me well would probably describe me as a tough individualist, a risk-taker and a free spirit. I'm never happier than when walking the musical high wire and singing hand-biting, *ohmigod*, white-knuckle, fall-off-the-seat arias at big-time events to packed stadia and arenas. Even at concerts, I'd pick pieces that hung off the far proud, purple edge of my range. *That* was my comfort zone. That's where I wanted to go. That's where I needed to go. I wanted to take myself to those sounds where I knew that, if they felt like a struggle at home in my hall, then, galvanised by the buzz and adrenaline that a live audience gives, I can belt it out and hit those high money notes loud and clear. I didn't want to spend the rest of my life singing 'Sixteen Tons'. And I certainly never want to weigh sixteen tons ever again.

From that moment, I was on a mission; I was determined to reverse the clock, fold back the years and return to where I once was. I think most people were aware that I had scaled down my repertoire to suit my then current disposition. However, the words of the man in the third row resonated in such a way, almost like a red rag to a bull, that I couldn't get them out of my head. *He's not what he used to be.* I went to bed that night still thinking about it. I woke the following morning. *He's not what he used to be. We'll see about that.*

First, I needed to find out what was wrong with my voice. Why wasn't it working? What was happening to the infrastructure? Had the steroids and the replacement hormones had some kind of long-term effect?

The following morning, I rang Patrick McGuigan – and we arranged to meet.

*　*　*

As I drove the twenty miles from Wilmslow to Northwich, I reflected on what had happened in my life over the past years, all of the ups and downs and where they had left me.

'Haven't seen you in a while, Russell,' said Patrick as he led me into the sitting room of his cottage. Retired in 2009, Patrick still taught privately. I was grateful he had agreed to see me.

'Let's have a listen, then, shall we?'

I began with scales. *La-la-la-la-la-la-la-laaa!* . . . Halfway though the scale of F, I glanced at Patrick. He wore an expression of Jesus-Mary-and-Joseph-what-has-happened-here? He raised a hand.

'Thing is, Russell,' he said, readying himself for an important speech. 'You have been through the most turbulent time with your health. What you've got to remember is, it's not just about what's going on here . . .' he pointed at his throat '. . . a high percentage of what you do is about what is going on in here,' tapping his temple with an index finger. 'What we've got to do is get your confidence back. When we get your confidence back for the higher line notes, that's the point when we will know whether or not you can do this stuff.'

Patrick put me though vocal boot camp. Painstakingly, over two or three meetings a week for several weeks, we began to build up the scales to the point where I was hitting the high notes, if not always cleanly. An A flat still had a bit of a croak, or I'd split on the top, or I'd hit it but put it into the wrong position, or I'd cover it instead of singing it open. I found I was unable to facilitate the process in the right way, as if I had forgotten how to sing.

'Let's try one of the easier arias,' said Patrick. 'Volare'.

No great pianist, Patrick could knock out a tune. At least, he knew the notes and was strict about the order in which they were played. As he plinked out the opening bars of Domenico Modugno and Franco Migliacci's hit single, which gave Italy third place in the 1958 Eurovision Song Contest, I felt an unaccustomed nervousness rise inside me. I launched myself into the piece and was doing okay, until I reached the bit at the end that rises to an A.

'*Volare o-o-o, Cantare o-o-o-%*&*@# . . .*'

'Let's try that one again, shall we?'

Off he unhandily plinked. I approached the climactic ending . . .

'*Volare o-o-o, Cantare . . . \$%^&* . . .*'

I stopped. 'I can't do it, Patrick. I just can't.'

'You can. Just try it.'

'I can't. It's closed up.'

'Confidence, Russell. Just hit the bloody note.' Patrick hit the lid of the piano for emphasis. It was the only time I heard Patrick swear.

I tried again. '*Cantare o-o-eugh*&^%! . . .*' The note folded on me like a cheap Kabuki Drop.

'Sounds more like a throat infection than an aria,' I joked weakly.

I felt embarrassed. Was I wasting Patrick's time? Was I wasting my time? He could see that I lacked confidence and technique. Maybe what had happened to my health had affected me more than I thought. Perhaps what I heard as the split and croaking note on a scale, he heard as a sad and hopeless cry for help.

Back home, standing in my hall, I rode up and down the scales, striving for the high notes but falling just short. Why did I lack the energy to hit and sustain the high notes? I didn't know which was worse: that I couldn't do it, or that I didn't know why. It seemed a task beyond impossible. Whenever I tried, I felt dizzy. My voice had vertigo.

Meanwhile, other voices in my head, each one singing in a sinister minor key, called out as if a Greek chorus was stuck between my ears: one was telling me I lacked confidence; another was saying I'd never sing properly again; and then there was this bloke telling everyone, 'He's not what he used to be.' As these withering denunciations rang in my ears, I thought, *Why can't I do this any more? I've had an operation on my brain not my effing throat!* Why *can't I do it?*

Alone in my hall, I wept bitter tears of frustration. The memory of the man in row three and my inability to hit the high notes, combined with everything else that was going on in my life – or not going on – seemed to have struck something very painful deep inside me.

I spent hours singing scales to the staircase, each note corresponding to a higher step; I serenaded the mirror, my primary audience, with arpeggios; I quavered vibratos to the front door. I wanted to be able to go back to Patrick and tell him confidently, with a straight face, 'I can do this. I have got my confidence back. I can sing these notes. I can do this repertoire.'

If art thrives on technical difficulties, mastering the great tenor arias of the classical operatic repertoire represents a supreme artistic achievement. They pose awesome challenges that only a tiny handful of people on this planet have the necessary range, power and control to overcome. They have an immensely refined aesthetic. 'Absolutely wonderful' is only a smidgeon away from 'pretty awful'; 'nearly right' might as well be completely wrong; the difference between brilliance and the bin can be as little as the wrong kind of wobble on a vibrato or a slightly flat note. Tiny, tiny things don't just matter a lot – they mean everything.

Take 'Non ti scordar di me' ('Do not forget me'), which Ernesto De Curtis, the Neapolitan composer, wrote in 1912, with lyrics by Libero Bovio, and which Luciano Pavarotti made look easy at The Three Tenors concert in Los Angeles in 1994. It is a minefield littered with the crushed egos of former tenors through which you have to play hopscotch. When Pavarotti performed it in 1994, he, as usual, made it look like a roll around in the hay. And yet to place it so that you keep your larynx in the right position requires a strategic approach a little like navigating a vocal obstacle course. Posture, head pos-ition and breathing are crucial elements of good vocal reproduction. And then you also must stay relaxed.

What may look straightforward to the audience is the sum of a hundred and one little things that have to be done just so and in the right order. When going for a really high note, I sometimes slightly twist my head to one side to elevate it slightly. It works for me anyway. I have watched video clips of my younger self singing and thought, *how did I hit that note with my chin resting on my chest? I would never do that now.* I'm not consciously thinking about all these things at once. Muscle memory kicks in. Well, that's what had happened in the past, but clearly something was failing to kick in now. Singing is an endless apprenticeship – perhaps I had lost sight of that. Even when I sing my last ever note, I will still be learning, still trying to improve.

12

MY WAY

AFTER FOUR WEEKS of singing to an audience of household furniture and the back of my hallway mirror, I rang Patrick excitedly.

'I'm hitting an A flat.'

I sped round to his cottage, trying to hold that evanescent A flat in my mind.

'Let's have a listen,' said Patrick as he welcomed me in. 'Quando le sere al placido', he said over his shoulder as he led me into his sitting room.

Damn! I thought. He was chucking me in at the deep end. One of opera's most famous minefields occurs near the end of the second act of Verdi's *Luisa Miller*. A lengthy leave-taking opens up to a lyrical aria of great classical beauty. It includes a series of A flats. Marked *appassionatissimo*, it demands great vocal heft, a firm line and a bright sound. Only a world-class tenor at the top of his game can bring it off.

Addressing the piano, Patrick gave me one of those cheesy professional grins that conductors of classical orchestras reserve for soloists who are about to launch themselves into a career-defining recital requiring awesome virtuosity.

I thought, *He is one man sat at a piano, but I feel more nervous singing to Patrick than to a packed Royal Albert Hall.* He had set the bar high. I desperately wanted to sail over it. I desperately *tried* to sail over it.

'Thing is, Russell,' said Patrick, closing the lid on the piano and possibly foreclosing my career. 'As we get older, the vocal folds deteriorate. You can no longer do what you used to do as a young man. When you started out, you could hit high B and high C for fun. As you age, those notes get harder and harder . . .'

A good example of a voice that has deepened with age is Elton John's. In his early recordings, his light pop-y voice soared. It had the most beautiful sound. Now, deeper and more resonant, it is equally lovely, but not as high-resting as it was. That's what happens with age. I couldn't disagree with Patrick, but still . . .

'You can't hit those high-wire notes any more. You have to accept that.'

I began to burn inside.

This. Isn't. Why. I. Am. Here.

I am here because I do *not* accept that, I fumed to myself.

I could not accept that, on the one hand, Patrick told me that singing is a confidence thing, and on the other hand told me that it is to do with age. These statements seemed at odds. Which one was it?

In my early career, I doubted so many things about myself, but if anyone said anything negative about me my toys left the pram. Now, more mature, I decided to underreact. Unlike the bloke in row three, Patrick hadn't thrown down a gauntlet or waved a red flag. He wasn't trying to undermine me. He had simply stated a few facts based on my performance. In the politest possible way, though, I still wasn't going to accept them. Nothing that I needed seemed to coincide with what Patrick was saying.

When I said goodbye to Patrick that day it was for the last time. I was hitting a solid if sometimes unreliable high A natural. At times, I'd stick on an A flat instead. It wasn't where I needed to be, but it was a big improvement on 'he's not what he used to be.'

I have often reflected on the manner in which Patrick and I parted company. I think he was trying to be kind to someone whose voice he felt had peaked and was on the way down. He was trying subtly to tell me that I was never going to be what I was before. He was trying to bring me down gently. I didn't want to hear that. Not yet.

My craving for positivity overruled reality. Of course, Patrick was correct. I wasn't getting any younger. The voice naturally deteriorates with age after a certain point. There's no recovery from the quiet attrition of time on flesh. I had no right to expect to be able to sing the way I did when I was younger. I knew all this was true, but I didn't like it. Like so many other times when I have disliked and declined reality, my zest for life and love of singing refused to be suppressed.

So, to paraphrase Frank Sinatra, I did it my bloody way.

There's probably a psychological term for it, something like amplification of commitment or plan-prolongation bias, when you decide on a course of action, despite mounting evidence that you are wrong and the plan is flawed, and yet, the greater the body of adverse evidence, the more determined you are to see it through. Ultimately, you have to take responsibility for these things yourself.

As I drove out of Patrick's driveway and headed back to Wilmslow, the inherent absurdity of my position didn't escape me. While the bloke in row three was right, Patrick, the legendary vocal coach to opera stars, was wrong. How profound is that?

* * *

'We're gonna get you in the biggest show on the planet.'

'We'd like you to appear in a musical: fifty grand a week.'

'We want you as guest artist at the Grammys.'

'Here's an idea I thought up in the bath.'

Many of the agents, managers, impresarios and middle men who got in touch were time wasters never to be heard of again. Sifting for gold is among the hardest parts of show business. Often – in fact nearly always – gold and sand are interchangeable. So many genuine projects drawn up in good faith go wrong, usually because money runs out.

Meanwhile an agent introduced me to a film company who were interested in producing a film about Mario Lanza, who had died of pulmonary embolism at 38 after suffering addictions to overeating and alcohol. I can't imagine why they chose me for the part.

This project was more than just the brainwave of some-one sitting at home in their pyjamas bashing a laptop. Nor was it dreamt up by two producers just before they keeled over in the pub. It was generated by credible individuals with solid backing, track records in movie-making and the right connections. Discussions were held, plans drawn up, a script drafted and so on. Result: silence.

I heard of another idea to produce a film about my own life story. This came from BMG, the Bertelsmann-owned

Santa Monica-based music company. The guy on the phone was all over it. 'What an amazing story! What you've been through is incredible!' Result: ditto.

In another project, I was asked to play God in a musical. The minds behind this spent hundreds of thousands on pre-production. Kerry Ellis and I were signed up along with a host of fabulous singers. They set up a press day and, prematurely I thought, began to book arenas. I even began practising a few of the songs. Then the money . . . You're ahead of me.

I try to be pragmatic when things fall through. I'll believe it when I'm on stage singing it and the money has cleared.

I once discussed this with my wife Louise when a particularly golden-looking opportunity vanished.

'Aren't you disappointed?' she asked.

'No. It was never there in the first place. It's all chat, just an extension of the ear-pleasing white noise that the industry pumps out these days. It's meaningless.'

However, in 2009 a call came in that seemed so unlikely it had to be real.

'Hi Russell, strap yourself in. I've got news for you.' It was Mark Cavell, my champion at Decca and then Epic. 'Benny and Björn from ABBA are doing this musical. It's been massive across Europe and Sweden. They are transferring it from Swedish into English. They want to know if you'd be—'

'Yes.'

'—interested. They have been running workshops in America to find someone with the range.'

'Yes. Yes. Yes.'

'They just want to see whether you can sing the part,' he said, 'whether you can hit the notes. *I* know you can. I think Benny just wants to sit around a piano with you.'

'I'm up for that.'

'Up' scarcely conveys the sense of hunger and fire-in-the-belly craving that came over me. My first thought was: *Oh my God, I really want this.* When Benny and Bjorn come knocking, who wouldn't want to rip the door from its hinges?

I began hoping, guessing and hallucinating that, if I could pull this off, it would assuage a thousand stinging slights from the music industry and perhaps help me pick up my career where I'd left it before my brain tumours hit. However, I was paranoid about leaks. Several times in my career, I have been harshly reminded that nothing travels faster in the universe than rumours of star-spangled job opportunities in the music industry . . .

Manager: I've just heard Russell Watson has been asked to do a gig.

Talent: What? Why haven't we been asked?

Manager: Dunno. Shall I make a call?

Manager, calling promoter: Why hasn't my client, who has sold more records in the last two years than Russell Watson, been asked to do this gig?

Promoter: Oh well, we'll have a word . . .

. . . and the next thing I know, some other bugger has swiped 'my' gig.

Now I keep my lips sealed until the signature is on the contract.

Benny and Bjorn's musical was *Kristina från Duvemåla*. It's based on four novels by Vilhelm Moberg, written in the 1940s and 1950s, about a family's poverty-driven migration from Sweden to America in the mid-nineteenth century. When Benny and Björn's original, epic, four-hour Swedish version premiered in Malmö in 1995, it received a rapturous response and a ten-minute standing ovation. The music was compared to that of Franz Schubert.

In 1996, an abbreviated – but still thirty-nine-song-long – concert version was performed in Swedish in Minnesota. It was compared to George Gershwin's *Porgy and Bess* in scope; its music was likened to the scores of Rodgers and Hammerstein. Back in Sweden, it ran for more than 650 shows over four years, making it the second-longest-running musical in Swedish history. A CD of the musical performed by the original cast lingered in the Swedish charts for seventy-four weeks.

Some ten years after its premiere, *Kristina* was translated into English for a new production. However, Benny was struggling to cast Karl Oskar, the male lead. He needed a singer whose voice could encompass bottom E and high B flat. Few vocalists have such a two-and-a-half-octave range. Some have power in the lower register but weaken in the upper. Others have power and clarity on the high notes but lack the resonance lower down. For two years, Benny had been running workshops in America to find a Karl Oskar. No candidate could adequately cover the upper and lower extremes that the part demanded.

I was invited over to Stockholm to audition. Beauty pageants aren't normally my thing; you either want me or you don't. This invitation was different, however. It was equivalent to the 33-year-old Russell Watson being asked to sing at Old Trafford for the last game of the Premier League season in May 1999. I would do pretty much whatever I was asked.

After touching down in Stockholm, I was driven to the Rival hotel, a former cinema theatre on Mariatorget on Södermalm Island. In my chic room, I took in with approval the Mats Theselius armchair, the Gunnar Asplund desk chair, the faux fur throws, the quirky art, the black-and-white photographs and, charmingly, 'Björn' the teddy bear.

The following morning, Benny picked me up in his Porsche 4x4.

'Good morning, Russell,' he said as we drove off. 'It is very nice to meet you. I have heard your music. It is very good. I like it.'

'Thank you.'

'How did you like the hotel?'

'Yeah, it's lovely, thanks.'

'Did you sleep well? Was the bed comfortable?'

'Yeah, yeah.'

'How was your breakfast?'

'I had it on the balcony with a beautiful view of the waterway.'

'On the balcony? Quite cold this morning, no?'

'I'm from Salford. As soon as we see a bit of sun, the shorts and T-shirt are on. The eggs were cooked to perfection. It was all very, very nice.'

'So you like it. Five star, yeah?'

'Five star plus.'

'Good, because it is my hotel!'

We both burst out laughing and the ice was well and truly broken.

We drove on, chatting away. After a few minutes, I said, 'Nice car.'

'What do you drive, Russell?' asked Benny.

'Audi Q7.'

'The Audi Q7! That's the size of a hotel, Russell!'

'Well, that's what I've got, anyway,' I chuckled.

Further on, Benny said, 'Look over there,' pointing to a massive imperial-style building overlooking the canal.

'What? The hotel?'

'Yah! That's your car, Russell!'

We both burst out laughing.

Benny's studio in downtown Stockholm was a small, regular room in an unassuming building. In one corner stood an upright piano.

He sat down at the piano and asked me to sing 'In the Dead of Darkness'. This beautiful song from *Kristina* is technically very difficult: it leaps up and down the scale, switching seamlessly from falsetto to full voice and then crescendoing with a high B flat. This is a piece that demands control and agility.

Benny was very specific about what dynamics he wanted.

When the song starts, 'In the dead of da-a-a-arkne-e-e-e-e-e-sss . . .', he wanted a light, floating falsetto, slowly building throughout the piece to full voice.

As I got to the business and began to belt it out, I noticed Benny's shoulders were shaking up and down. He was laughing. We finished the song, he swung round on his piano stool, and said, 'When do you want to start?'

His two-year quest to find Karl Oskar was over.

In the playbook, Karl Oskar has been separated from his wife on board a ship crossing the Atlantic. One of his children has died and he is devastated at his loss. Benny wanted me to amplify the sense of anguish and heartbreak. The song's shifting dynamics were a perfect way to do this, but to bring it off was not the work of a moment.

Technically, it is difficult to combine falsetto with full voice. Falsetto drives more air through the vocal folds than full voice. I can sing full-voice A-A-A-A-A-A-A . . . for as long as I want; if I sing falsetto a-a-a-a-a-a-a-a . . . I soon run out of breath. The greater volume of air dries out the folds, which compounds the difficulty.

The same challenge but on a lesser scale occurs in 'Bring Him Home' in *Les Misérables*. It begins in falsetto and then switches back and forth between full voice and falsetto.

The high B flat of 'In the Dead of Darkness' then drops down to your boots, adding to the feeling of tackling a vocal assault course. Of all Karl Oskar's songs, 'In the Dead of Darkness' took the most work. It is a hell of a sing.

I was going to perform in the premiere of the English version of *Kristina* on 23 September 2009 at Carnegie Hall in midtown Manhattan. Helen Sjöholm, a fantastic singer and brilliant actor, who performed both in the original Swedish production and in the concert version in Minnesota in 1996, played the title role of Kristina.

The role itself was a massive undertaking and I spent months learning the part. I wasn't just singing solo numbers and duets, I was also heavily involved in the ensemble. I was proud of accomplishing all of this so soon after the turmoil of my second tumour and radiotherapy.

On the final evening at Carnegie, I literally poured every ounce of my heart and soul into the performance. I had this inner feeling that I was almost reliving some of the trials and tribulations of my own story. In the final scene, where Kristina dies in the arms of Karl Oskar, every tear that I shed was an out-of-body experience. It was beyond what I understood to be just acting. I have never felt like this before or since on any stage.

After the show we all stood chatting outside our dressing rooms. Benny and Björn had invited some friends and special guests along. Benny showed Helen and me over to a group of ladies he was chatting with. I did a quick double-take – one of them was Meryl Streep.

'Go on, tell him! Tell him what you said!' Benny said to Streep.

'Err, hello,' I said.

'Oh my God! It's Karl Oskar and Kristina,' said Meryl

Streep. 'You two – I said to my girlfriend while we were watching – these two have to be married! No one can act that married.'

Helen's husband watched on in horror.

'No, we're not married,' retorted Helen quickly.

It was one of the greatest, if not the greatest, endorsement of my career.

Benny is my kind of superstar: a super talented, down-to-earth man, who often wears his heart on his sleeve. He has a wicked sense of humour, similar to mine. I was, if you like, his 'baby'. He'd found me and brought me to *Kristina*.

When I changed my phone a few years ago, I accidentally wiped my contacts. If you are reading this, Benny, do drop me a line.

* * *

While preparations went on behind the scenes to produce *Kristina*, news of my recovery from brain surgery and my seeming return to form spread to Taiwan where, in July 2009, I was invited to perform at the opening ceremony of the eighth edition of the World Games in Kaohsiung.

These games cover sports not contested at the Olympics, including artistic roller-skating, rhythmic gymnastics, bodybuilding, synchronised flower arranging, aerobic sphincter clenching and bear wrestling – actually not those last three, which I made up, but you see where I'm coming from.

Six thousand athletes from one hundred and one countries took part. The opening ceremony was held on 16 July in World Game Main Stadium, a solar-powered five-storey 40,000-seater that looks like two hands reaching out to embrace the world. Four thousand performers took part in the ceremony. Themed 'Beautiful Island', it rendered 6,000 years of Taiwanese and aboriginal culture in words, music and dance, as well as motorbikes, Pili puppets (a popular local entertainment), street dancers and fireworks. It was the largest single event Taiwan had ever staged, watched by a television audience of 100 million. Somewhere into this programme, Hayley Westenra, the brilliant New Zealand soprano, and I were squeezed in to sing a few pieces.

Before we went on, Hayley and I were sitting in the 'green room', a pleasant enough air-conditioned lounge. When we were introduced, a great roar went up. We walked through a door and entered the stadium and . . . *What the . . .!* I felt like I was walking into the guts of a tropical hair drier. It was 44 degrees and 100 per cent humidity. I have never experienced heat like it. I even had to take my tie off. Blinking through the sweat,

Hayley and I duetted 'Pōkarekare Ana', a traditional New Zealand love song; 'The Prayer' and 'We Are the Champions' by Queen. I don't usually need a towel on stage. But that night I could have wrung my suit out afterwards. That night was among the best but also among the worst experiences I've had on stage. The euphoria of singing in a packed stadium again was incredible, but the heat – oh my word – I'll never forget the heat.

13

ESCAPISM

I WAS STANDING in my bathroom one evening when, in an instant, everything went ink black. It was my worst nightmare come true.

'Oh my God!' I screamed, as I fumbled my way around the topography of my bathroom, my heart trying to leap from my chest. 'It has happened! I can't see! I'm blind.'

I had dreaded something going wrong with my sight, a sure sign that the tumour was back. I had been previously informed that the size of my tumour could potentially lead to blindness.

'Don't worry Russ,' called Victoria from downstairs. 'The electricity tripped. It's all fine. Are you okay?'

My hysterical overreaction to a random occurrence may seem funny in retrospect, but it shows how much fear I carried in my head, and the hair trigger that sets it off. People who have suffered serious illnesses may sympathise. I remain hyper-vigilant about my health. A twinge, an ache or just a low-level sense of something amiss, and I panic. Luckily, Dr Tara Kearney, concierge and conscience of my physical well-being, is standing by. I feel fortunate to have her and her encyclopaedic medical knowledge available on speed dial. I expect she can interpret dreams and predict the future but I have never dared ask.

Cutting right across my heightened sense of hypochondria is a deep and abiding loathing for anything to do with hospitals. Some patients can't work out which is worse – the illness, the cure, the doctor's bedside manner or those monstrous upside-down faces staring at you while you lie on a hospital bed or table about to be cut open or have something shoved up or injected into you. For me, simply being in a hospital is bad enough. Just visiting Outpatients makes my blood pressure soar. The anxiety attack overrides the sedatives. A nosocomephobic (one who fears hospitals) hypochondriac seems like the definition of chaos. Hospitals are often part of the problem, not always part of the solution. I particularly hate MRI scanners and will do everything I can to avoid them.

I was never claustrophobic until I was fed into an MRI scanner with its eyes mapping and photographing me, and was told, 'You have a brain tumour'. That was it.

Hello full-blown, galloping claustrophobia. It strikes me in the most mundane ways. I once saw a television programme about a guy whose hobby was crawling underground in caves: 'Aaargh! Where's the remote?'

Every six months, I am meant to have my blood tested and every twelve months my head scanned in an MRI machine. I won't contact the hospital; I wait until they contact me. Even then I might not do anything about it. Sometimes Tara has to drag me kicking and screaming to the MRI unit.

One morning, my back seized up. I had no idea what was wrong.

Oh God I'm dying!

I'd lost control of my muscles and felt a searing blue pain shoot up and down. Mad scenarios flashed through my mind. As it is no longer able to generate its own stress hormones, my body cannot cope with stress. I began to cry. Shaking and weeping, I thought my life was crumbling around me.

I rang Tara.

'Something's really wrong this time, I'm going to die.'

'Calm down. Get a cup of tea.'

'I can't get a cup of tea. I can hardly move!'

'Okay, sit down then. What does it feel like?'

'I've got this pain in my back. I can't feel anything and I can't walk.'

'Where is the pain?'

'Left-hand side, near the base, just above the glutes.'

'Sounds like a slipped disc.'

She was right. A disc had dislodged and was out of position. A physiotherapist and course of naproxen sorted it out.

* * *

A side-effect of some steroids that I take is that they can make sleep difficult. This compounded an additional, paralysing, problem, which was that I had a fear of going to sleep that sprang from the time when my second tumour haemorrhaged while I was asleep. Going to sleep one night, only to wake surrounded by a team of para-medics saying, 'Stay with us, Russell', stuck the idea in my head that, if I fell asleep, I would never wake up and I would die. This was an idea that whirred around my head each time I went to bed. I was constantly thinking about death. *Am I going to die?* I would wake in the night sweating, my heart pounding, having to force myself to calm down.

So I was doubly sleep deprived, which certainly does not help the singing. I reached the point at which my sleep deficit overcame my general mistrust and fear of doctors. I made an appointment with my GP.

'Well, we can try you on some valium,' he said. 'That might relax you in the evening.'

Valium helped me get to sleep, but didn't *keep* me asleep.

When I mentioned this to a friend, he slipped me a zolpidem tablet. *Bingo!* I asked my doctor for a prescription. With much tooth-sucking and sharp intakes of breath, he agreed.

'But only for a short time,' he said, finger raised. He hedged his prescription with caveats and dire warnings about the risk of abuse.

'Yeah, okay,' I said.

The prescribed dosage of two and a half milligrams worked, until it didn't. By breaking the tablet in half instead of into quarters, I upped the dose to five milligrams. That likewise worked, until it didn't.

It is curious how these things steal up on you. Besides helping me sleep, up to a point, zolpidem also brought out a streak of low, animal cunning. I began to tell my doctor, 'I've lost the packet. Can I get an extra one?'

Meanwhile my friend began giving me his spares. I was able further to raise the dose to fifteen milligrams, and so on.

The doctor kept warning, 'You've got to come off zolpidem.'

'Yeah, but I'm still a bit stressed about this, and troubled by that, and I'm getting worked up about the other. I still can't sleep at night.'

Slowly, slowly, I learnt that you don't need to have an addictive personality to become an addict.

That wasn't the only hole I was digging myself. I was also hammering the booze, often three bottles of wine a night. I had begun drinking heavily when I discovered that the tumour had come back. Alcohol extracted me from my reality and helped distract me from thinking about it or pondering imminent death. One surgeon had told me that there is nothing like having a brain tumour to make everything seem worse. The booze was a form of escape.

In those days, being me didn't come cheap. I ran on top shit: Puligny-Montrachet, Condrieu and Krug Grande Cuvée. I was weight-lifting bottles of Pol Roger Cuvée Sir Winston Churchill. I was panning it. Grant Ainsworth was privy to much of it. When not recording and mixing, he would join me.

During one wind-down session of liver marination, Grant was sitting on the sofa watching television; I was in my chair. 'Thing is, Grant,' I said, as I exploded another bottle of Ruinart Blanc de Blancs and brought the fuming neck to his glass, 'You don't get the same hangover when you drink top-quality shit, even when pissed as a rat.'

When drunk, I don't get aggressive or teary or start dancing naked on tables. I simply turn into an even bigger idiot.

A large shag pile carpet lay between us on the floor. I decided to lie down on it and roll from side to side, laughing and talking gibberish.

'. . . I mean, we're talking transcendent grape juice here, mate, a liquid of such poise, finesse and balanced intensity that you won't get a hangover, and, if you do, it'll be a better class of hangover . . .'

What began as a vertical tasting of fine champagnes and first growths became a horizontal tasting of soft furnishings.

Grant sat watching television without paying the slightest attention to the grown man at his feet rolling around on the floor of his own house, talking nonsense.

The next morning, I went downstairs for breakfast. Grant was already there nursing a coffee,

'You all right, mate?' I asked.

'Yeah, mate. You? Good night's sleep?'

'Yeah, great thanks.'

'Everything under control?' asked Grant.

'Yeah. Brilliant,' I said. 'Oh, er, Grant, by the way, was I . . . was I rolling backwards and forwards on the rug last night talking gibberish?'

'Yeah.'

'And do you see that as normal behaviour?'

Grant looked nonplussed. 'Under the circumstances, yeah.'

Holy shit! I thought. *I need to do something about this. This isn't right.*

What with the vicious sleeping-pill habit and the booze, I felt I'd reached not so much a crossroads as a spaghetti junction on my Via Dolorosa from Salford bolt-cutter to UK's biggest-selling classical artist. My health difficulties were compounding and spiralling out of control. Some words of warning that Gerry, my step-grandmother, had once told me sprang to mind. She said that, as my piano-playing grandfather lay dying of drink on the floor of their prefabricated bungalow in Anglesey, he had told Gerry, 'God, I hope Russell never ends up like this. Make sure Russell never ends up like this.'

My grandfather was a full-blown alcoholic. He used to bury bottles of hard liquor in the back garden. At Gerry's insistence, he was banned from stores in the area. An engineer in the RAF, he had talked about a drinking culture. Warned that his drinking would kill him, he still carried on, and it did.

I started to rein in the booze.

Still, thanks to the zolpidem, I was getting at least *some* sleep. I wasn't quite ready for stopping that yet.

These weren't the best of times. I was exploring the dark side of the rock 'n' roll life. I find it hard to look back on this phase without being struck by the sheer unlikelihood of my meeting, never mind becoming the husband of, my wife Louise. It's a minor miracle that we got together.

14

LOUISE

ON THE EVENING of 19 February 2010, a group of pals arrived at my front door.

'Come on, Russ,' they said, 'let's go out.'

I wasn't keen. I was still in my antisocial phase.

'Honestly, Russ. Come on! Get out of your pyjamas, get dressed and let's go out.'

'Okay,' I said, reluctantly.

At Panacea, a clubby restaurant with a VIP lounge in Alderley Edge, a lady approached and asked if her cousin could take her photograph with me. Sure. I looked over her shoulder at her cousin and, seeing a beautiful young blonde, thought, *Blimey! Wow!*

Socially shy (no, seriously), I felt unable to ask her out, so I sent one of my pals over instead. She accepted.

When I met Louise, I had no ambition to be in a relationship; I'd had enough of all that. I was happy on my own. There is an age gap between us. When we started going out, some people said, 'That'll never work. She is with him for one reason; he is with her for one reason.' *Blah blah blah.*

A very caring, animal-loving person and dressage rider, she made me realise that I needed someone who is strong willed, but not jealous. If you are in the public eye and have a life partner, wife, husband or whatever, it is imperative that they support you. If your partner doesn't support you, you will get endless grief. I've been there. Done that. Got a drawer full of T-shirts.

From that meeting, our bond developed and strengthened. Soon Louise became a constant in my life. On Christmas Eve in 2013, I drove her to one of our favourite picturesque spots, a green that we had visited on the previous Christmases. In the middle of the green there is an old tree, under which we would take a selfie together each year, which has since become a tradition for us. That year, however, I had something different in mind. It was late at night and freezing cold. When we got to the tree on our walk, I got down on one knee, produced a ring, and asked Louise to marry me.

The service and ceremony took place in 2015 in Benahavis near Malaga in southern Spain, followed by a reception at Restaurant Valparaiso on the Costa del Sol overlooking the sea. The choice of Benahavis was for the weather. Louise had said that she didn't want to have to

'Put a brolly over my dress if we had a wedding in Congleton and it rained.'

I was so nervous about giving my speech that I couldn't eat the wedding breakfast.

'Come on babe,' said Louise, 'you've sung for the Pope and in front of millions of people on television. And here we are having a wedding in front of one hundred people. Calm down.'

My mother-in-law had to take me for a walk to calm me down.

At the time that we met Louise was working as an administrator in a company, a job that she loved. In 2017 she began to work for me, as an interim, as my assistant Victoria had by this time moved on. Seven years later, she is now my manager and business partner. She plans all my shows and concerts one year in advance, handles all my social media and acts as my go-to sounding board. She accompanies me on eighty per cent of my concerts, but, as she looks after our menagerie of horses, chickens, lambs, dogs, alpacas and Fuzzy the South African ostrich whom she rescued from a zoo, Louise is a reluctant long-distance traveller. She is someone in whom I can trust. After fourteen years together, we have built a great life. We're best mates.

When we started going out, Louise asked, 'Why do you keep shaking your head like that?'

'Like what?'

She rocked her head from side to side.

'Oh, that. I'm just checking.'

'Checking what?'

'Checking that it's not come back.'

'That what's not come back?'

'The tumour.'

I could feel it rattling inside my head. Although officially 'removed', a small souvenir of the tumour remains, which is partly why I have to submit to the much-dreaded annual MRI scans – to check it out and make sure it remains Nessun dormant, as it were.

Still, even after Louise and I became an established couple, I preferred to stay at home. The social agoraphobia that began in 2005 continued to haunt me. Getting me out of the house was like trying to pull a goldfish from its bowl. Going out for a meal was almost unheard of. To compensate, I tried domesticating myself by learning how to cook. One evening, I offered to prepare dinner for Louise: potato gratin, green beans and a delicious steak cooked medium rare with a red wine *jus*.

'Wow!' said Louise, when I served it. 'How did you make this?'

I gave her a detailed account of the pains that I had taken in order to conjure the ultimate potato gratin '. . . a dash of this, a drizzle of that and a *jeuje* of the other.'

A few weeks later, Louise asked me to cook the same dinner again. Once more, I produced a great feast. Unfortunately, Louise happened to glance into the rubbish bin. I then had to explain the great lengths I had gone to in order to perform my potato gratin-ectomy from its Marks & Spencer plastic packaging and place the delicacy in a serving dish.

'The accompanying red wine *jus*, however, was all my own hand.'

Louise agreed that the red wine *jus* was indeed 'the best thing you cannot buy off the shelf.'

A year into our relationship, Louise said, 'You need to go out more, babe. You need to be doing stuff. You need to be seen. You're sat at home all day in front of the television. You are wasting your life.'

She was right. Like a mad celebrity recluse, I had shut myself away in darkened rooms festering while watching daytime television. Very slowly, I began to go out. I even drove Louise to the Four Seasons Hotel in Hampshire for a luxurious break. We had the spa and 500 acres of pastoral scenery almost to ourselves. Still, we dined in our room.

15

BACK TO WARP SPEED

Show business is famously unforgiving. You have to fight your way in thick fog up a long, slow, muddy, potholed gradient, littered with broken glass and bodies, and studded with status quo bollards. You are in constant danger of falling off a cliff. Even when I announced that I was back on my feet and ready to go, the industry's appetite was weak. I felt I was seen as a liability.

During 2009, Sony began making overtures. Ged Doherty, who grew up in Wythenshawe near me, and had drummed for various Manchester bands, ran Epic, Sony's pop label. Ged was keen to get me on to Sony's books. When I visited Epic's offices to meet the team, they were all up for it. In December 2009, I swung a superb deal with Epic. The impetus came from Mark Cavell, my champion at Decca, who had lately jumped ship to Sony. Among all the record company executives

I've dealt with, Mark was my greatest supporter and most passionate advocate. In my early recording career, he was an important influence. I always felt he had total faith in me – a feeling that was reciprocated. He's a cheeky chappy who likes a drink, a laugh and a chat about football, and he and I naturally got on.

Sony/Epic is a very different beast to Decca. Decca was excellent at selling and packaging classical crossover. Sony were going to package me almost like a pop artist.

It's unusual that a best-selling recording artist should switch labels in mid-career. This was no light-touch friendly hand-over. As soon as the ink had dried on my shiny new contract with Sony/Epic, music industry fun and games took on an edge.

In January 2010, Decca released *With Love from Russell Watson*. This easy-listening introduction to old and new pieces was nailed together using tracks from previous albums. Sold in petrol stations, it notched up 90,000 sales, despite having no promotion.

Meanwhile, I began recording *La Voce*, my debut album with Sony/Epic. It was predominantly a classical album. It was recorded live in Ennio Morricone's Forum Music Village Studios in Rome with the 75-piece Roma Sinfonietta. My first real recovery and return to form following brain surgery felt like a very emotional home-coming. You can hear this in tracks like 'Parla piu piano',

Mascagni's Intermezzo and 'Someone to Remember Me'. Many people commented on the strength, richness and vibrancy of my voice, which sounded like it had matured since my brain operations. In fact, although I had struggled with it for so long, my voice seemed to have improved significantly.

That *La Voce* was recorded live made a big difference. I always perform to a higher level when singing live than during the mix 'n' match of recording passes in a studio. The snag with live recordings is the expense. If anyone makes a mistake, you have to go back and re-record, unlike in a studio where you can excise the error, record a replacement and insert it in the gap.

I can usually tell if an album will fly or flop while I'm recording it. The signs are always physical: goose bumps, a tingling feeling, hairs on the back of your neck bristling, that sort of thing. Why or how they come about is a mystery, but these 'tells' are sure indicators of quality. I knew *La Voce* would be a hit long before we had finished recording it.

In November 2010, seven days before *La Voce* came out, Decca released *The Platinum Collection*, a 'spoiler album' of mainly recycled and re-packaged opera and pop numbers that I'd recorded, as well as a few tracks that never made it on to earlier albums. Remarkably, it shifted 210,000 units.

A spoiler is an album that your former record label releases to 'spoil' the launch of your debut album with your new label. The idea is to cannibalise sales and distract attention. Decca owned the rights to an entire library of my recordings. They could do with these tracks whatever they pleased. In the run-up to Christmas that year, *La Voce* and *The Platinum Collection* slogged it out against each other. *La Voce* notched up 220,000 sales. That year, across the board, I sold over half a million records over the counter, which was unprecedented for my genre of music.

* * *

One very pleasant interlude in 2010 occurred in late June. Francis Yeoh's YTL Corporation invited me to sing at Muse Hotel's grand opening party in St Tropez. Yeoh is the Malaysian plutocrat whose vast sprawling interests include Wessex Water, two-thirds of the electricity of Singapore, various hotel chains and the island resort of Pangkor Laut in Malaysia. He even holds some of the rights to 5G. He is crazy wealthy. Fortunately, he has a soft spot for classical opera that dates from his friendship with Luciano Pavarotti. I met Francis when he asked me to sing at YTL's fiftieth anniversary celebration, alongside a number of stars of classical music, to an audience that included the King of Malaysia and the great and good of Kuala Lumpur.

With its terraced gardens and white-and-cream palette, Muse was *the* address in the summer of 2010, probably still is. Five minutes from Place des Lices, it lies a short Bentley ride from the beach at Ramatuelle. Among the performers at the party was George Benson. Rehearsing for the opening show, I sang 'Nessun dorma' while George watched. As the final note rang out across St Tropez, George leapt up.

'Holy shit! Where the fuck does that voice come from, man?'

'Thank you.'

'What a voice. Where you from?'

'Salford.'

'What the fuck do they put in the water over there? I gotta get myself some of that shit right now.'

* * *

By the end of 2010 I felt like I was finally beginning to emerge from the long shadow that two brain operations had cast. Having kicked the biscuit habit and eased off on the booze, I had made peace with the mirror and was back down to my fighting weight. Now having Louise in my life made a big difference.

Still, my body and my moods were behaving strangely. Some days, I would wake up shouting, 'Let's go!' and feeling like I could run the London Marathon backwards. Other days, I'd wake up feeling like the weight of the world had landed on my shoulders and I wanted to jump off a cliff. I felt I had no self-worth, and didn't want to go out anywhere or do anything or see anyone. I have since learnt that my mind and body need to exercise and stay active. As soon as I stop, dark clouds descend and darker feelings take over. If I don't get any sense of achievement during a 24-hour cycle, I feel flattened.

I need to feel in some way relevant. If I sense a lack of relevance, I begin to feel that everything in my life is stopping. This is the wellspring of my work ethic, and was especially so in my early career. I felt I couldn't say 'no'. I didn't want to risk becoming irrelevant. Slowly, I have found a way of controlling this insecurity, thank God. Without that control, I'm sure I would have burned out. Even so, if I go for four months without appearing on television, radio or in the press, I start to think that people will forget about me and that part of me no longer exists.

Likewise my voice wasn't performing properly. Its form was sporadic. At some concerts, I would come off stage thinking, *Wow!* At others, I'd think, *Oh my God, what has happened? The strength has gone.* I think many of my vocal issues were interrelated, by-products of my various health battles. This sometimes made me nervous about singing the big classical arias. If I felt something amiss or if I'd done several concerts in quick succession, I knew that I would struggle. This had a toxic and compounding knock-on effect. The pressure to perform can so easily lead to greater pressure and self-doubt. If anything goes wrong, and if social media pick up on it, the pressure increases exponentially. Very soon, you find yourself down a deep, dark rabbit hole of doubt and anxiety.

The question I am most often asked, even more frequently than 'When did you first start singing?', is 'Do you get nervous?'. The answer is always, 'No. Never.' Besides my wedding day, the only times I have ever felt trepidation or nervousness is when my voice was under-performing. This matters because confidence is the sovereign value of all performing artists.

If you struggle with a specific note during perform-ance, it stays with you. If I'm singing 'O sole mio' and I don't hit the top note in the way I would want to, the next time I sing that note that memory will stick in my head when I am performing it. Even if I know that I can hit it as clean as a whistle, I'll be thinking, *Oh God! Last time I hit that note, I messed it up.* Before you know it, you have a rolling nightmare on your hands. It is the same when you stall during a section of dialogue during musical theatre. Your brain gets hung up on it.

When singing the operatic repertoire and the Neapolitan arias, unless you have the mindset to think, *I am going to blow this note away and make it look easy,* you will fail. I can make it look easy because I've navigated the vocal obstacle course umpteen times. The classical repertoire is a real vocal work-out. It is considered art. Those arias were deliberately written to be very, very difficult. You must be at your peak. You need absolute confidence in your own infallibility.

*   *   *

To say I 'never' get nervous is perhaps a slight, but only very slight, exaggeration. I once lost my cool. In my early career, I established a reputation for performing at some of the biggest sporting events in the world, to packed stadiums. It's something I enjoy and seem to be good at. I keep getting asked, and I don't get nervous.

In 2002, however, I was invited to perform at the opening ceremony of the Commonwealth Games in Manchester. I was due to sing 'Where My Heart Will Take Me', which Diane Warren wrote for the 2001 series

Star Trek: Enterprise. This is the only Star Trek series with a vocal soundtrack and I had the honour of singing it.

Waiting to go on, I was standing next to a steward.

'You all right there Russell?' he asked.

'Yeah. You?'

'Yeah mate. Aren't you nervous, going on in front of all these people?'

'No, I'm okay pal.'

'The stadium is rammed, mate. There's 40,000 people out there!'

'I'm cool with that.'

'I mean, what with all the athletes from all the nations surrounding yer,' he continued, 'holding the banners in the air. And the Queen being there. Don't you get nervous?'

'No, no. I'm okay with that. Still cool.'

'And I've heard,' he persisted, 'that there are one billion people watching live on telly.'

'Right, that's enough now. Now you are making me nervous!'

* * *

Still popping zolpidem, I met Tara one day at the hospital for a coffee.

'So how are you feeling at the moment, Russell?' she asked. 'Do all your levels feel okay?'

'Everything feels normal,' I replied. 'Actually, it feels nice, after all this time, finally, to go to bed at night and not think I'm going to die.'

Tara looked at me in horror. 'Pardon?'

'I mean it's nice, finally, after two years, to stop thinking about dying every night.'

'You are telling me that for the last two years you have gone to bed fearing that you will die?'

'Yeah.'

'You're mad. That's how you felt?'

'Yeah.'

'And you've not spoken to anyone about it?'

'No. It's just shit, isn't it? Didn't think it was important.'

Tara nodded her head as if this was really very serious. 'You should have spoken to someone about it. There is a name for your condition: PTSD.'

'Well, I've stopped now.'

'That epitomises your outlook on almost everything, Russell. You analyse things internally.'

'I dislike burdening people,' I said. 'Sometimes, when I have spoken out about things, I've asked myself, Are these people really interested or are they pretending? Will they use my words against me? Will they see me as a liability? In my line, weakness or even vulnerability can be provocative.'

I never told Tara the extent of my sleeping pill habit. I was more concerned that if I came off zolpidem I wouldn't be able to sleep and my worst fears of dying would come charging back. DIY amateur psychotherapy was never my strong point, so I kept quiet about it. I think Tara suspected that I was exceeding the prescribed dosage, but she would have been horrified by how much. She certainly had no idea that I had been hammering the booze too.

I know. *What a twat.*

16

WHITE COAT PHOBIA

I'm ALL ABOUT (cliché alert) the emotional journey, with a few ticks and photo ops on the way. In 2010 my itinerary looked superficially like a dazzling *tour d'horizon* of fascinating and exotic places. I only stopped off at home to refuel. God or Mother Nature or (for atheists) the randomness of biology, however, kept trying to throw obstacles in my path.

Green Hedges, my then local tennis club, was located in a converted RAF aircraft hangar. I can't pretend I was feeling match fit that summer's day when I turned up anticipating the usual straight-sets thrashing by my coach. In fact, I felt like I was going down with something. *Never mind,* I thought, *I'll sweat it out over two sets.*

As soon as I set foot on the court, I was all over it. Everything was working, forehand, backhand, an incredible slice. Normally I could never get near my coach. This time I was giving him a real game. I was the young Roger Federer incarnate.

I got home, had some food and began to feel like I had indigestion. I went to bed thinking, *This hurts.* It felt like somebody was pushing their fist from the inside of my chest out. My pulse was pounding. The pain would just not go away. I later got up, still hurting, and drank some milk. When friends who were staying over saw me the next morning, they said, 'My God! You've gone grey.'

'Yeah, I feel grey, like really bad indigestion. I've had pains in my chest all night. They won't go away.'

When I rang and explained to Tara what had happened, we agreed that I should go to the hospital to get checked out.

'Tara, I'd like you to come with me, for a second opinion.'

'Okay.'

As soon as Tara set eyes on me, she dropped an expression that she clearly reserved for emergencies. 'Oh my God, Russ! What's going on? This looks really bad.'

Staring down the barrel of another health alarm, I was put on a bed, and wired and tubed to monitors and drips. Blood samples were taken. Victoria and Grant, who had come along with Tara, stood beside my bed watching gravely. White as a ghost, morphined against pain, I was as high as a kite. Honestly, the stuff you come out with when you are on morphine! I put my hand down the front of my pants, looked at Tara and cried, 'Holy shit!'

'What?'

'My balls are massive!'

The specialist at the hospital entered the ward waving papers at me. 'A miracle has happened,' he said. 'You should not be alive. Any doctor looking at these charts would immediately assume that you had had a massive heart attack. You have a condition called myopericarditis. You have a swelling of the heart and the heart sac. Your enzyme levels are almost one hundred times higher than normal. We've never seen them so high. We sent your blood samples back to the laboratory because we didn't believe what we were seeing.'

I felt a white-coat homily coming on.

'You need to relax now. You need to take it really, really easy,' he continued. 'This is very serious. Your heart has been attacked by a virus that has got into your bloodstream. I need to insert a stent into your groin, then move it up to your heart to keep one of the valves open. It is blocked.'

His voice sounded to me like an autopsy. Tara looked on, concerned.

'You gonna operate, then?' I asked.

'Yes.'

Instinctively, my eyes looked for angles of escape. Nature seemed determined to avenge her failure to kill me with the 'second' tumour. Red fire flared behind my eyelids; my brain took flame. White-coat phobia blazed inside me. I burned the specialist up with my eyes and uttered a rosary of expletives. I wanted to scream so loudly. Talk of operations stressed, frustrated and frightened me. As the specialist wandered off, I said to Tara, 'This is going to kill me. And if it doesn't kill me, I might do something regrettable.'

'*What* is going to kill you?'

'This.' I waved my arms in the air. 'The humming machines, the bright lights, the people walking around wearing white gowns, gloves and masks . . . Just being in this environment freaks me out. A police cell would feel more welcoming. I've been through enough. I just want to go home. I don't want to be in hospital.'

'The thing that is more likely to kill you right now is your heart,' said Tara.

In almost all circumstances, I am perfectly capable of restraining myself. I can usually listen to reason. But in this instance, I decided to take firm, decisive and rash action. I sat up, unclipped the wires, tubes and cables, got out of bed, pulled on my clothes and walked outside.

'What are you doing?' said Tara, her voice a pleading treble. 'Where are you going?'

'I'm going home. I'm not having another fucking operation.'

'You can't. You are as close, if not closer, to death with this as with your tumour. You are lucky to be alive. Many don't come out alive with this condition. The survival rate is not good. Your heart is—'

'Yes, but is this a prison?' I asked.

Tara gave a cross-bearing sigh. 'That's so stereotypically you. No, this is not a prison, Russell.'

'So I can leave when I want.'

'Theoretically, yes.'

'Well then, I'm leaving.'

'But you can't.'

'You just told me it's not a prison and I can leave when I want, so I can, and I'm going.'

'What are you going to do?'

'I'm going to go home.'

'And do what?'

'Recover.'

Tara dropped a *where's-the-straitjacket?* look of alarm. 'You are in hospital! *This* is where you're recovering.'

'I'm sick and tired of being in hospital and having operations. I'm not having any more. I'm going home.'

Tara resisted the temptation to say I needed my head examining. She did, however, say, 'You're mad.'

'Then I'm mad. I'm going home to be mad.'

With the kind of sure recklessness with which I have managed to get away so often in the past, I was determined to do it my way, go rogue if necessary, even if that put me on a collision course with Mother Nature and biology. Once again, I refused to let reality, or the logic of a medical diagnosis, get the better of me.

Tara, failing to appreciate the genius of my strategy, drooped, and gave me a look of reproachful sorrow. 'There's optimism, Russell, which we know you are good at and which we all love, and there is a healthy disregard for the noise of battle, but there are also delusional levels of wishful thinking and sheer bloody-mindedness. And . . . and . . .' Tara seemed to run out of steam. Then she rallied and made her point. '. . . I'm just trying to save you from yourself.'

Not without considerable difficulty, I managed to harden myself against Tara's words.

Gary pushed me in a wheelchair to the car. I got in and we headed home.

Tara rang every few hours.

'Are you okay? Is everything all right? Are you stable?'

'Yeah, I'm fine. I'm okay now that I'm home. I feel much more relaxed.'

The next day, against the advice of the entire medical fraternity, I climbed aboard my cross-trainer, strapped on a heart monitor, and set off. *What a dickhead.*

One ... Two ... Three ... Four ...

Within four steps, my heart rate shot up to 198 beats per minute. I stopped, recovered and went downstairs. The next day, I did the same. This time I managed five steps. My heart pounding away at 190 beats per minute, I dismounted. I repeated this exercise every day, slowly building up stamina. Within six months, my heart rate seemed to have recovered. Going against all medical advice, while carefully monitoring my heart and keeping my pulse under control, I regained my health.

Seven months later, I allowed myself to be subjected to an MRI scan on my heart.

'This is not possible,' said the specialist, staring at me as if I'd dropped from the clouds.

'Pardon?'

'This is not possible. This is not the same heart.' He produced my previous scan and compared the two. 'Look at the scar tissue here.' He pointed to the early scan. 'And look here.' He pointed to the new scan. 'Almost gone.'

I did another scan. Same result. The specialist could scarcely believe his eyes.

My main concern was still playing on my mind, however.

'Is it all right if I play tennis now?'

'Yes,' he laughed. 'You can carry on as normal. Just take it easy at first!'

Let me be quite clear, I'm no advocate of self-medication, especially if you are diagnosed with myoper-icarditis, especially if like me you have a serious sleeping pill habit and are on steroids and prone to attempting to manifest Roger Federer on a tennis court. It really was very irresponsible. I do realise that. With hindsight, I would have been better off had I had that thing shoved up my groin. But I was still going through PTSD and feeling the trauma of not waking up after my haemorrhage.

Now, along with all the other list of stuff I have to keep on top of, I have ECG check-ups with Tara.

Tara has often told me, 'You were very, very stupid. You could have died.'

Would I do the same again if it happened tomorrow? No. Well, maybe. I don't know. Mad, stubborn or canny? All I'll say is that our capacity for deluded optimism while blinding ourselves to unwelcome truths, and our trust in hope over experience, probably lies at the heart of human achievement. It could be our saving grace.

In contrast to the second brain op episode, I wanted no one to know about the heart scare. All I had running through my mind was people's response to my two tumours, and the thought that I was considered a liability. I suspected that the music industry regarded me simply as a white-noise generator, a wind-up toy, a set of replaceable moving parts. If the product is faulty, it is unsellable. That was me.

I never discussed my heart episode with family, still less friends. And I certainly wasn't going to let anyone in the music industry know, although news has a habit of leaking out. I could almost hear a whispering gallery of discontent and pained disgust growing louder, as critics reached for the handbags.

'Now what?'

'Oh, it's his heart this time. Myopericarditis. Ever heard of it?'

'No.'

'Supposedly he nearly died again.'

'Oh God! First of all it was his throat, then it was his brain, and then it was his brain again, and now it's his heart. What next?'

'If he was a cat, he'd be dead by now.'

'He's become a liability.'

'He's hit the floor so many times it's a joke.'

'We're deep into Monty Python territory.'

'A notice of cancellation comes with his CV.'

'His autobiography will be required reading for aficionados of health catastrophes'

'If he survives to write it.'

I didn't want to be pigeon-holed as a liability. I didn't want the suits and the critics to caper and keen and generally rub their hands together with glee at another Russell Watson health scare. Until this heart episode, I felt I was getting back on track. I decided to keep quiet and just deal with it.

Having to cancel an entire tour didn't help. Between late 2010 and 2011, I had to call off so many shows that I was an insurer's nightmare. In the first half of 2011, I did one tour uninsured. Had anything gone wrong, it would have been goodbye Prometheus, hello Icarus. The dashboard puppy would have been roadkill.

17

DISTINCTION WITHOUT
A DIFFERENCE

ON A MORE positive note, I finally managed to kick
the sleeping pills habit. I went about it in a typically
'me' sort of way. Louise and I were settling into our
first class seats as guests of Francis Yeoh, ready to fly
to Pangkor Laut, his resort-island off the Malaysian
peninsula.

'Would you like a newspaper, sir?' asked the cabin
steward.

'Yes please.'

I glanced at the front page headline. It shrieked about
sleeping pills being a possible cause of early onset
dementia. Zolpidem loomed large.

'Oh my God!' I said to Louise when I showed it to
her.

By now, I had been taking zolpidem for several years.
I was popping twenty milligrams every night, eight

times the prescribed dose. If you took that amount from a standing start, you'd soon be dead.

I. Never. Touched. Zolpidem. Again. It was a case of 'Goodbye sleeping pills; hello Horlicks.' I swear I quit – there and then.

If I'm doing something, anything, that isn't right, that is stupid and silly and an abuse of health, even though I know it isn't right, I might still do it. But when someone says, 'You are an idiot. You shouldn't be doing this,' I stop. No questions asked, no ambiguity tolerated, no grey area trodden, no climb-down negotiated, no fade permitted. Just stop.

Considering the role that 'Nessun dorma' (translation: 'None shall sleep') has played in my career, reputation and personal experience following two brain operations, if I'm knighted it will probably be for services to the sedatives industry.

On that holiday, I destroyed what zolpidem I carried with me and I didn't sleep for virtually the entire trip and for nine nights after. When I finally was able to doze off again, my brain came up with lurid polychromatic and stereoscopic dreams and anxiety scenarios.

I made an appointment to see Tara once I had returned home.

'Hey, guess what?' I said.

'What?'

'I've stopped taking sleeping tablets.'

'Fantastic! How did you do it?'

'Just stopped.'

'What?'

'I just stopped,' I said, snapping my fingers for emphasis.

'Do you know how dangerous that is? You are supposed to wean yourself off sleeping pills!'

'I just saw an article saying that the sleeping pills I was on are linked to early onset dementia and I thought, well, I don't fancy that, so I just stopped.'

Tara scanned my face as if looking for signs of intelligence.

'Why didn't you call me first?'

'Pfff.' I gave her my best, rugged, take-me-as-I-am expression. 'You know me. I'm not qualified to receive medical advice.'

'And how were you?'

I shrugged, paused and finally came up with, 'I was sweating. Couldn't sleep. And when I could . . . Well, you can probably imagine what it is like living with my mind . . . I had all sorts of weird visions and monsters chasing me.'

'Russell,' she said, shaking her head slowly, 'I'm beginning to wonder if they removed the common sense lobe as well as the tumour.'

When not despairing at my cavalier attitude, Tara seems to regard me as an inexhaustible source of amusement and entertainment.

'Unfortunately, I don't have a medium setting,' I explained. 'It's all or nothing, I'm afraid.'

It was ironic that someone normally so in control of their professional life and so careful about their public persona should spiral so wildly out of control and in the wrong direction. The booze and the pills were intended as coping mechanisms to deal with, respectively, the pain of my second brain tumour going symptomatic and my fear of dying in my sleep. They were also means of escape. They played a role that performing on stage had served in healthier, happier times. I realised that performing live to a packed audience is my comfort zone and my safe space, and I needed to understand and respect this.

*   *   *

Not long after I came off the pills I was invited to perform in 'A Salute to Vienna', a one-off at the Wiener Konzerthaus in Vienna, one of the most famous concert halls. Frederica von Stade, the American mezzo soprano, sang Vilja's aria from Franz Lehár's *The Merry Widow*. The Symphony Orchestra of the Volksoper Vienna played the 'Thunder and Lightning Polka' and 'The Blue Danube' by Johann 'Waltz King' Strauss II. It was an all-acoustic performance, so no microphones. Backed by the Volksoper orchestra, with its flawless execution, my voice soared as I sang 'Dein ist mein ganzes Herz' from the 1929 operetta *Land of the Smiles* by Lehár and Fritz Löhner-Beda.

You are my heart's delight and where you go I long to be.

The clubs of the North West have nothing on the Viennese when it comes to critical scrutiny. Audiences don't come much tougher. The place erupted.

There is nothing like an Austrian or German orchestra. Along with the Japanese, they are the most clinical. If you listen to 'Ride of the Valkyries' from *Die Walküre* by Richard Wagner played by a German or Austrian orchestra, there is no back-phrasing or laying off the beat; every note is bang on the beat. Put it on in your car and you feel like you can rule the world. American orchestras have a beautiful flowing, fluid tone. Italian orchestras are all that you want from them. Italians own the greatest opera music, which they play with joy and a sense of romance. Despite the odd wrong note, Italians wear their hearts on their sleeves, and you can hear that in their music.

A couple of years later, in July 2015, I sang in a UNICEF concert in the Terme di Caracalla in Rome.

On this particular night, the Caracalla was the setting for an awesome evening held al fresco with free entry to a crowd of thousands of Italian opera fans. I shared top billing with Andrea Bocelli, José Carreras and Cynthia Lawrence, 'Pavarotti's favourite soprano'. Even Ben-Hur would have been impressed.

I went on directly after José Carreras. José was lovely. Andrea Bocelli was incredibly charming, as was Veronica, his wife.

The concert felt like a throw-back to the good old days of the full-on, set-piece, epic mega-event with multiple joined forces and lavish trimmings. More than anything else in my career, I miss those massively extravagant shows with lights, orchestra and packed houses. Such spectaculars as the UNICEF concert have become prohibitively expensive. If you look at the leading lights in classical crossover and the majority of classical performance artists who sell large numbers of tickets to the general public, not many of them use full orchestral accompaniment any more. It's so hard to get large events involving full orchestral forces to pay for themselves, let alone turn a profit. Something of this scale was only possible thanks to the munificence of Francis Yeoh, who in June 2015 donated one

DISTINCTION WITHOUT A DIFFERENCE

million euros to Teatro dell'Opera di Roma and took a seat on the board. He wanted to put on his own welcoming party.

It is always daunting to sing in Italy to Italians in Italian, but 'O sole mio' and 'Volare' got a marvellous response.

Afterwards, Cynthia Lawrence came over.

'Oh, my God!' she cried. 'Your voice! *Che fantastico!* Oh my word! Amazing! Do you perform in opera? *Ti esibisci nell'opera?*'

Cynthia had no preconceptions. She just judged me on what she heard coming out of my mouth.

'No. I do concert tours.'

'Ohmigod! I had no idea you weren't Italian.'

'I'm from Salford.'

'Right. Over here, they're crying out for voices like yours. You would be perfect. *Perfe-e-e-e-tt-o-o-o-o!* Good looking, tall, dark, handsome. The ladies would love you!'

She had little idea who I was and simply saw me as I seemed: a bloke on a stage singing.

* * *

My finest Italian moment came in 2016. I travelled to Rome to record live with the Roma Sinfonietta in a glamorous studio in the centre of the city. When we finished, some of the instrumentalists got up, walked over to me, slapped me on the back, pinched my cheeks, poked me in the tummy and said things like, '*La tua voce è fuori scala, molto potente. Sono rimasto davvero sbalordito.*' (Your voice is off the scale – really powerful. I was really blown away.) and '*Hai una voce fantastica che può cambiare da canzone a canzone: dall'opera classica, passando per il romanticismo e il rock, fino al pop e a Broadway. È incredibile e cantato con tanta emozione e chiarezza!*' (You have a fantastic voice that can change from song to song: from classical opera via romance and rock to pop and Broadway. It's amazing, and sung with such emotion and clarity!)

They spoke so fluently and fast that I had to say, '*Scusa, parla più lentmente. Io sono inglese.*' ('Sorry, please speak more slowly. I'm English.')

'*Ah, inglese!*'

'*Si. Di* Salford.'

[Blank look.]

I felt more complimented by them thinking I was Italian than by what they were saying.

18

BILL BOWS OUT

In December 2015, Bill Hayward, my old vocal coach, musical director and mentor, died of cancer. Ever since my second brain operation, Bill had become increasingly peripheral to my career, mainly due to his own health struggles. Yet even when he was unable to conduct me, he'd say, 'I want to get better so I can get out on the road and do some more concerts with you.' I was equally desperate for him to do so.

The last time we met in person was in Shrewsbury in 2015. I was performing at the Severn Theatre. I had invited him to the concert and said it would be lovely if we could meet during the interval.

'Bill is in the lobby,' said Louise when I came off stage at halftime. 'He's a bit unsteady on his feet. I think you should go down to him, babe. He doesn't look good.'

I went down to the lobby to look for a large man with an ample girth and his usual smiling face, but I couldn't see him anywhere. *Where is Bill?* I thought.

'Russell, Russell,' came a voice from behind me. I turned round and there was Bill. He had lost so much weight that he hardly looked like himself. He was unrecognisable. I only knew it was him through his voice. It was heartbreaking.

'I know,' he said. 'You always said I should drop a few pounds for the sake of my health. I have just gone about it in the wrong way.'

After that evening, we spoke a few times on the phone, but I found it increasingly upsetting. There was an inevitability about it all. Bill kept saying he didn't have long left, that he had had his time but he would take so many fond memories of our times together with him. I was trying to convince him that the Royal Albert Hall beckoned, and he needed to get better for that.

'Oh Russell, you're always the optimist. How I wish,' he said in what was what was to be our last telephone call together. I think we both sensed that. It was utterly devastating.

At his funeral in January 2015, I paid my respects and sang 'Panis angelicus' by César Franck. It was a miserable day outside. It was grey, it was raining; there was almost like a mist in the air. It was the type of day that Bill wouldn't have liked. I began to sing the aria and by the time I'd got virtually to the end – probably the last two lines – the most amazing thing occurred, almost like some kind of divine intervention. The whole place lit up. You could see everybody physically looking around: 'What's happening?'. The sun had come out and it was shining through the stained-glass windows. It was remarkable. I immediately felt this sense that Bill was there with me. And the tears just flooded. I was sobbing like a child. I didn't get to the end of the aria. Everybody stood up and clapped. They'd all felt the same thing. I think they'd all felt the same presence. Bill was there with us.

Bill always called it as he saw it, no matter what about or to whom it had to be said. In one of the first recording sessions we did together, I was singing with the Royal Philharmonic Orchestra. Bill sat in the control room. More familiar with live performances and opera than with recording studios, he had just discovered the intercom button, which allows the control room to speak directly to the conductor, who was quite well known. Halfway through 'Panis angelicus', Bill came over on the intercom and the conductor stopped the orchestra in mid-flow.

'Yes, Bill?'

'Bar sixty-four. Do you know that there is a parallel harmony there?'

'I'm aware of it, yes. What's your point, Bill? Why have you stopped the entire Royal Philharmonic Orchestra mid-flow? There is nothing wrong.'

'Well, there's a parallel harmony.'

'And your point is, Bill?'

'Well, quite simply, it's a rookie's mistake. The strings and the wind were playing the same line of music when they should not have been.'

The orchestra, who could hear the conversation, cracked up laughing.

The conductor darkened. 'Bill. Outside. Now.'

They both went outside. Words flew. The conductor returned red-faced. Bill resumed his post in the control room: 'He told me not to interrupt him again,' he said. 'But – just being straight, just being honest – it's wrong. Shocking breach of purity. That sound you just heard was César Franck turning in his grave.'

When Bill began giving me singing lessons in the late 1990s, I promised him that one day I would repay his generosity. I am so glad that I had the chance to fulfil my promise. His dream had always been to conduct the Royal Philharmonic Orchestra. When I did my first run of big concerts in the UK off the back of *The Voice* I was booked to perform at the Royal Albert Hall. As he was my musical director, I rang Bill to give him the news.

'Have you got your baton ready, Bill?'

'Yes, it's always ready for you Russell. What have you got planned?'

'First and foremost, we are going on tour.'

'Lovely. Lovely.'

'The pinnacle of the tour will be the Royal Albert Hall. You will be conducting the Royal Philharmonic Orchestra.'

'Yeah, yeah, whatever.'

'That's what we are doing.'

'Yeah, okay Russell, whatever. Stop fooling around. It's not funny.'

'Seriously, you're going to be conducting at the Royal Albert Hall.'

'Really?'

'Really.' The phone went quiet, except for the sound of Bill breathing. 'Are you all right, Bill?'

'Yes. Yes, I might just have something in the corner of my eye, Russell. Both eyes, actually.'

Performing in the Royal Albert Hall to a sell-out audience of 5,500 was incredible for me, but it was Bill's moment, Bill's day, Bill's dream. It's one of my favourite memories of him.

Bill was the most important person in my career. This may sound strange, but of everyone whom I have lost, family, friends and colleagues, were I to have the chance to speak to anyone in heaven, it would be to Bill. I miss him that much.

One thing always gnawed at me about Bill. He never

once said, 'Russell, you're amazing'. I know. It sounds pathetically needy of me, but it was something I always wanted and strove to attain. Bill's approval meant everything to me.

After a performance, he'd say things like, 'Yes, wonderful Russell, good stuff. Really lovely . . . Yeah, you were good tonight, you did a good job . . . You sang really well.'

I always felt there was a momentary hesitation, a slight check, in his praise. I craved more. I always sought his absolute, unqualified approval.

Six years after Bill's passing, a longstanding fan sent me a group of photographs; it was basically pictures of Bill and I together. One of them shows me holding a microphone and I'm about to sing at a concert. Bill's stood behind me, with his conductor baton in hand poised and ready, looking over his shoulder at me. It is more than just a smile. It is also a look of approval, even admiration. He was where he wanted to be, with the person he wanted to be with. The photograph was all the confirmation I needed. Pride was written all over his face. My eyes fill up every time I look at it.

Thank you, Bill.

19

'BEANS ON TOAST!'

AFTER BILL, WE lost Patrick McGuigan in 2019. Someone else who challenged me, helped me improve and believed in me was no longer with us. Richard Thompson, my long-standing agent who represented me around the time of my operations and recovery, had moved on to sports promotion. All my creative champions who were at Decca and Sony have moved on too. It's not like I'm bereft of a good night out; I am lucky to have plenty of pals and I still have fun. The difference is that I no longer have industry pals to talk to at length, and I enjoy a good natter. I sometimes feel lonely. Besides Louise, who tends to see things in black and white, and remembers absolutely everything except that I tend to change my mind, Alistair Gordon, rock 'n' roll legend turned music producer and father of two daughters, is probably my main audience.

There is always Aled Jones, of course.

I've known Aled since about 2000 and have recorded three albums with him. I can't say we're bestest friends. We don't go out on Saturday nights drinking beer together. But we know each other well enough and I'd say I trust him. It is always good to have someone in the industry you can trust. Aled is . . . how can I put it? . . . He's probably not what you'd imagine him to be. He's actually quite funny, a proper giggle. After a couple of drinks, we're like two children. In fact, we're fairly infantile even sober.

We had been talking about this and that and generally shooting the breeze one day in 2018, and soon afterwards he wrote to me, half-jokingly, to say, 'We should do something together.'

I wrote back in the same spirit: 'Yeah, all right. Let me know when.'

The next thing I knew, his management was on the phone to Louise, planning a tour, an album and various spin-offs, sideshows and promotions.

The process was almost unbelievably quick. Spin forward a few months and we were in a studio making an album, with a tour already mapped out. Even in the studio, I could tell that *In Harmony* – a relaxing, 'feel-good' selection predominantly of hymns, with a few secular classics, accompanied by the New Zealand Sinfonietta – would be a hit. We launched to an audience that had an excellent appetite. It sold 120,000 units, a remarkable number in that market and at that time.

To promote the album, we did dozens of joint interviews. Being Welsh, Aled has an accent and diction that is, well, Welsh. I startled at something he said in a particular phone interview when he was talking about the 'blend' of our voices in *In Harmony*.

When the interview closed, we chatted on the line during a five-minute break before the next interview.

'Aled, did you just say "bellend", then?'

'What?'

'You sounded like you said "bellend" in that interview. "Well, you know, the *bellend* of our voices is really good."'

This was an opportunity too good to miss. In our next interview, we decided to see how many 'bellends' we could fit in.

'Yes, I think the *bellend* of our voices is so pure and clean, don't you, Aled?'

'Ah yes, Russell, you know, you can't get by without that *bellend*.'

'Yeah, it's just the perfect *bellend* of two voices. They just *bellend* so well together.'

It was hard to tell if the poor presenter from BBC Radio Wherever twigged.

* * *

I always study the work of tenors and other singers. If I spot a nuance or trick of their voice that I like, I might try it on – for fun and to see what it feels like, how the sound works.

Pavarotti, Domingo and Lanza are pre-eminent in my pantheon of tenor deities. When I sat outside Pavarotti's dressing room waiting to rehearse with him and Charlotte Church for Picnic with Pavarotti in July 2001, I said to Charlotte, 'I've not been this excited since I met Father Christmas.' I meant it.

There have been times when I have been compared by the press to these greats. Which is lovely and all, but I take everything written about me in the papers with a healthy dose of scepticism. One article in the *New York Times* said, 'He sings like Pavarotti and entertains the audience like Frank Sinatra.' I take things like that with a pinch of salt – it's lovely to receive that kind of praise, but no, *I wish*.

Another of the world's best tenors, Andrea Bocelli, divides opinion. A fabulous musician, he is far from your stereotypical tenor. His is not a full-blown operatic voice. Compared to Domingo and Pavarotti, Bocelli adds sexiness. If you listen to him singing 'Una furtiva lagrima', from Donizetti's opera *L'elisir d'amore*, and then listen to a classical opera singer, Bocelli's semi-nasal quality produces a sound that has a pop lilt, while still being classical-esque. I think that is why he is successful. He is easy to listen to. That is not to criticise classical singers who sing fabulously. But for a mainstream audience, Bocelli produces a commercial sound that is perfect.

Nat King Cole's warm, woody voice has a bit of a rasp at the back. It comes from his throat and mouth, not his chest. 'Unforgettable, that's what you are . . .' has a lot of air around it. It's hardly a clean sound, but it is a beautiful one. Remarkably, Nat King Cole's recordings sound like they were done yesterday.

A wonderful interpreter of music, Frank Sinatra was a brilliant back-phraser. In 'Fly Me to the Moon', for example, he lays off the rhythm and the beat. Instead of 'Fly me to the moon', he will sing, 'Fly me [slight pause] to-the-moon'. It sounds like he is taking liberties with the tempo; in fact, what he does takes great skill.

Whitney Houston's voice is in my opinion unparalleled for its range, power, and almost incredible pitching intonation. Maria Callas is another one of my favourites. She was a true diva who produced a beautiful, lyrical, effortless sound. Perfectly phrased and articulated, her 'O mio babbino caro' from Puccini's *Gianni Schicchi* will make you cry.

Sometimes, I find myself imitating singers who are associated with particular songs. Mike Moran and I were recording 'Nature Boy', which eden ahbez wrote in 1948.

(ahbez's real name was George Alexander Aberle. A hippie, he slept outdoors and for a while camped beneath the first 'L' of the Hollywood sign in Los Angeles.) The song was first and most famously recorded by Nat King Cole in the same year.

'There was a boy . . .'

But as I got to the end of the next line – 'Russell! You're going into Nat King Cole.'

In recent years, as my singing technique has improved, I've managed to avoid imitating other singers. I have found my own space. But my accent still shifts around. This adaptability has come about partly through necessity. Call it snobbery, but you really cannot present classical music with a Salford accent. If I walked on stage in the Royal Albert Hall and announced, 'You awright our kid? Me next piece is, er, "Nessun dorma" by, er, Puccini and wha' 'ave yer,' people would laugh or think I was taking the mickey.

Of course, when I go out with my friends, I naturally slip back into the Salford accent and diction, especially after a few drinks . . . 'You know, like, if I was talkin' to me mates and wha' 'ave yer, that's kinda like 'ow the accent goes, you know what I mean, our kid?' That's Salford. You don't pronounce the 't's and wha' 'ave yer.

Even so, there has been a shift in my 'natural' accent. If I've not seen my friends in a while, one of them will usually say, 'Tell yer what, our kid, yer accent 'aven't 'arf changed over the years.'

'Do you think so?' I'll reply, slipping into Michael McIntyre. 'I mean, personally, I don't see it myself. I don't recognise it. I think I sound just like you. But if you say so.'

*   *   *

I was once chatting to a soprano I have sometimes performed alongside. Hers is a fine voice with all the power that you want from a performer.

'May I make a suggestion?' I said, after one performance.

'Of course. I'd actually really appreciate it.'

'You've just sung "O mio babbino caro".'

'Yes.'

'This aria is the female equivalent of "Nessun dorma". When you sing it, what are you thinking of?'

'I'm trying to get into the thought process of . . .'

'Do you know what it means?'

'Yes. It is about a woman's love for her father.'

'Kind of. It means "O my beloved father". But you are not performing in the opera; you are singing an aria. Think about something that you can relate to. Think about your own father. That will induce a certain emotion, maybe too much emotion. But think about something you can relate to in the context of the song. It will give you the passion and energy to infuse something into the music that isn't quite there.'

'Right.'

'The other thing is when you begin the aria, lighten it a bit . . . 'O mio babbino caro' . . . so that when you go u-u-u-up to the high notes, they sound more effective. Callas offers the perfect example. The light and shade in her voice is immense. She gives it a bit of rock and roll, and something *real* that goes beyond what is written on the page. She infuses it with her own personality. She often got criticised for it.'

The advice I gave her was a rather more considered, strategic and I hope helpful nugget than that imparted to me when I was starting out as a concert performer.

Deke Arlon, an old manager of mine who was a *proper, like, facking sarf-east Landan geezer,* used to look after rock and roll bands *and stuff loike vat.* Deke was a character. Had he not been tied by the restrictions of his employer Sanctuary plc, Deke could have been a fabulous manager. He knew the business inside out, partly because he had played a significant role in creating it. I think he would have done well for me.

A vibrant character with an aura about him and swept-back grey hair, he was a Denmark Street legend who broke into the music scene in 1959 as Deke Arlon and the Tremors. He went from performing to publishing to producing to managing. Among his charges were Sheena Easton, Jerry Rafferty, Cher, Rod Stewart, Lulu and Celine Dion. He guided Elaine Paige's career for twenty years. He was the most old school manager I've worked with. He walked the walk and he talked the talk. Most people in the industry knew him. He was known for being hard-nosed and no-nonsense.

During our one year together, I did back-to-back concerts at the Royal Albert Hall. Each one ended with 'Nessun dorma'. In rehearsal, I blasted out the final high B, . . . *Vince-e-e-e-e-rò* . . .

'Kabuki down!' shouted Deke in impresario-director mode. 'Applause, applause, applause. Russell goes off stage left. More. More. More. Russell comes back on. *Encore!* It's a wrap!'

A Kabuki screen is a floating curtain that falls down in front of the stage from a specially erected metal frame. It was one of Sanctuary's brainstorms. It cost a fortune and was quite a work of construction. I mean, when you have such a beautiful stage as at the Royal Albert Hall, why cover it up with a giant metal frame covered with a giant pair of knickerbockers? And why obscure the organ and its magnificent pipes with a giant backdrop of me? It reeked of maximum expense for minimum effect.

Deke came over. 'Russell.'

'Yes Deke.'

'You know when you hit the last note of "Nessun dorma"?'

'Yeah.'

'Can you at least make it look like it's a facking effort? 'Cos you are hitting this note that only a few people on the planet can, and you're stood there, like, you know, you're flippin' a facking coin for 'eads or tails.'

* * *

Pavarotti, Domingo, Lanza, Bocelli, Nat King Cole, Sinatra, Houston and Callas all have high emotional IQs. More importantly they have a mysterious X factor that connects powerfully with the audience, that can cross fire and water. This connection is absolutely essential.

If you could put your finger on what gives a voice or a singer or even a character connective quality, and if you could describe it scientifically and then reproduce it, record labels would do so every day. It is indescribable and unknowable. You can't go around with a tea strainer catching it. All objective judgements about performers have to be done by reflection: when I sing to an audience, the emotion that the music conveys moves the audience, who reflect that emotion back. I can go on stage on a Tuesday night and sing 'Caruso', and something inside me connects the sentiments of the words and music to the audience. I feel emotional and get goose bumps. Sung well, 'Caruso' doesn't need translating. It's obvious what the words mean and I can tell this by the audience's response.

Te voglio bene assai [I love you very much]

ma tanto tanto bene sai [but very, very much, you know] . . .

Still, the audience may respond in a way that on the following night they might not, and that in turn will raise my game, which affects the audience and so on, in a series of micro-reciprocations that form a virtuous circle that is essential to a great performance.

It is hard to know where or how it all begins. The audience knows when you are connected, but if you stopped and asked them, they probably couldn't say why, and nor can I. Why I'm connected to a certain song on one evening but not on another, even though I go looking for it, is one of the nameless mysteries of singing. It is one of those strange, unknowable somethings that forever crowds the artist's mind and yet about which he or she is almost wholly inarticulate. None of it makes sense, thank goodness.

The half-dozen or so great classical arias that form the core of my repertoire are pieces that, depending on your mood, will inspire you, move you to tears, possess you and sometimes drive you mad. They are mother lodes of emotion. I cannot think of another art form that can so rapidly have people welling up within a minute and blubbing within two other than a well performed operatic aria. These arias represent a world of values beyond the power of logic to express, and whose full power can only be felt not understood.

There are, in my opinion, three great Italian opera composers, Puccini, Verdi and Mascagni, of whom Puccini is my big, bouncy therapy castle. It is difficult to explain how romanticism is depicted or comes across as music, but if you were wanting an example of how that happens, all you have to do is listen to Puccini. It is all there.

His writing for the voice is brilliant. He understood the voice and knew what tenors need in order to do their job. Unlike some writers today, he wrote sympathetically to the vocalist. He grasped the importance of open vowels, notably the 'ah' sound, when singing high notes. For example, when you reach for the high C in the aria 'Che gelida manina!' in *La Bohème*, Puccini has helpfully added a little step up, which is perfectly written for a tenor. 'Recondita armonia', the first romanza in *Tosca*, where the hero Mario Cavaradossi compares Tosca, his love, with a portrait of Mary Magdalene that he is painting, is another example: this very tough aria is helped along by the big, open vowels that Puccini wrote.

Ironically, 'Nessun dorma' offers very little help in this department. It climaxes on a closed vowel, the 'e' of *vincerò*, a difficult vowel to sing high, made more difficult by the prior sound of 'ch'. Many tenors find a way of slightly embellishing it to produce a more open vowel sound. Patrick McGuigan would say, 'Open up the "che" sound to make it almost an "a-a-a-a-a" instead of an "e-e-e-e-e"? This is what Pavarotti does. The word means "I will win". Maybe Puccini felt like he should throw down a bit of a challenge.'

* * *

I recently went on tour to Scotland. The evening before we set off, Mike Moran stayed over. I've always been very interested in the Queen catalogue. Freddie Mercury and I have one thing in common: we have a very wide vocal range; we can sing very high and very low. At one concert, I was taking a break while Mike Moran played 'Love Of My Life' on the piano, a sentimental ballad from Queen's 1975 album *A Night at the Opera.* I thought it sounded great and mentioned it to Mike afterwards. I became intrigued by it. When Mike stayed over before we set off for Scotland, we went into the music room. I asked him, 'Can we have a run-through of "Love Of My Life"?'

So off we went.

A few minutes later, Louise came in.

'Hey Louise,' I said, 'Listen to this.'

With Louise standing next to me, I began to sing, and – I don't know why – but the atmosphere went from *quite emotional* to *very emotional*. At the end, Mike turned round to me. 'Fucking 'ell, Russell. That is off the scale remarkable. I've not heard it sung like that in a very long time.'

As a performer you need to feel emotional about what you are singing, but I am very aware that too much emoting can ruin a performance. If I feel myself welling up, I say to myself, 'Beans on toast! Beans on toast! Beans on toast! The power of beans on toast! My friend beans on toast! Beans on toast are my middle names!' That usually brings me back into the room, but I mustn't overdo it otherwise I might have a fit of the giggles.

20

BACK TO REALITY

THE PRODUCERS OF *I'm a Celebrity ... Get Me Out of Here!* had tried to get me on the show a few times over the years, but I had always resisted. When I got another invitation in early 2020, to go on the show in the autumn of that year, Louise encouraged me to do it. Normally we plan a concert tour for the autumn, but we agreed it could make sense to skip it for one year. And what a fortunate decision that was too – for this was the year of the pandemic and the lockdowns and we would have had to cancel all our gigs anyhow.

Because of Covid the twentieth series of *I'm a Celebrity ...* was the first not to be held in Australia. It was to be shot somewhere even more remote: Gwrych Castle, in Abergele, North Wales. I'm still unclear how you pronounce 'Gwrych'.

However, there was an additional consideration. For me, the most challenging part of going on *I'm a*

Celebrity ... wasn't the privations or the horrible challenges that the producers dreamt up. It was the medical examination.

I may have addressed, and even come to terms with, many of my body's and mind's caprices, and I may have discarded the unhealthy 'coping mechanisms' that I'd devised, but I still feared doctors, hospitals, clinics and anything medical. Asked to submit to a full check-up, blood test, blood-pressure test and echocardiogram with a doctor in Harley Street, I found the very words 'Harley Street', 'doctor', 'blood-pressure test' were quite enough. My blood pressure soared: 186 over 98.

'I'm sorry, Russell,' said one of the producers. 'There is clearly an issue here. We can't allow you on the show. The insurance company would never sign off on those numbers.'

'My blood pressure isn't normally that high,' I explained. 'It was only high because I was having it tested by a doctor in a clinic.' Amazingly, the producer seemed to accept this twisted back-to-front logic and I was allowed to have a second blood pressure test at home, which turned out okay.

When you enlist for *I'm a Celebrity* ... strict rules apply. Contractually sworn to secrecy, you mustn't discuss it with anyone. When Ruthie Henshall, the Olivier Award-winning actor, singer and dancer, and I travelled by Land Rover to Gwrych Castle one grey, damp day in mid-November, we wore balaclavas so that no one would spot us. All part of the 'experience'. We arrived at a muddy holding area clustered with prefabricated huts. The door of one hut had swung open to reveal a foul, fluorescent-lit loo.

'Look at those disgusting toilets,' I said to the assistant producer who was escorting us.

'I know,' he replied. 'They are the ones we have to use.'

I tut-tutted and shook my head. 'I don't envy you that.'

'Yeah, they're awful.'

Like me, my fellow contestants were grateful for the chance to escape from, and perhaps temporarily forget about, Covid. As Shane Richie, the actor, put it, 'We're unemployed entertainers.'

We all got along. Beverley Callard, the *Coronation Street* actress, emerged as the mother figure, a lovely person and easy to get on with. I already knew Vernon Kay, the radio and television presenter. He is a bundle of fun and a good laugh. Shane Richie and I became better friends after film-ing than during filming. Jordan North, the BBC Radio 1 presenter, turned out to be a real character. Ruthie and Beverley were the ones I connected with the most. Hollie Arnold, the paralympic javelin thrower, was lovely too. We were a multi-talented bunch of slight misfits.

The most impressive contestant was Victoria Derbyshire,

the BBC journalist and television presenter. She had a way about her and seemed to know what she wanted and how to get it. She wasn't prepared to put up with nonsense. She came across as a very powerful lady. I liked her. Ever since then, I've seen her on current affairs programmes firing awkward questions at politicians, which suits her down to the ground.

I was bunked next to Sir Mo Farah, the great long-distance runner. Mo slept in a hammock next to my bed, which was an iron grate. The slightest of men, very thin and super-muscly, Mo exactly lived up to my expectations of what a long-distance runner should look like. His body mass index must be about two.

Each night, he zipped his sleeping bag up over his nose so that his eyes peeped out over the top.

One night, he said, 'Rock me, man. Rock me, Russell. Rock me.'

'I'm too tired tonight, Mo.'

'No, rock me, man. Please rock me.'

'Oh, all right.' I stuck out one foot and gave his hammock a half-kick, half-push.

'Faster. Faster. Faster,' he screamed.

So I kick-pushed him harder.

'Faster, faster.'

The hammock looked like it was about to rotate and do a full circle.

'Mate, I don't want to be responsible for breaking the legs of the fastest long-distance runner in history.'

'Come on man, please.'

'No. That's it now! Good night.'

This is surreal, I thought. Where else but on *I'm a Celebrity . . .* would you get Britain's best-selling classical artist lying on a metal grate next to one of the world's all-time fastest long-distance runners, while engaging in what for all the world appeared like a parent pushing a child on a swing.

I cannot describe how disgusting our dunny was. We had a dribbler among us too. Someone literally was pissing all over the floor. The place stank. Nobody ever owned up to it but we all had our suspicions.

My fellow contestants kept urging me to sing, but I struggled. I had no energy. Our rations were tiny. I have never felt so hungry. In seventeen days, I shed twenty pounds. I could feel the weight tumbling off me.

Our diet consisted mainly of dried rice, which we had to soak overnight, and beans. The beans tasted of less than nothing, if that is possible. It was the most taste-free diet I have ever experienced. The water tasted disgusting too, like wood-marinade. It was warm, which made it worse. On one trial, I spotted a giant flagon of fresh water in one of the holding areas. Great! I filled my canteen.

253

Afterwards, I told me fellow contestants, 'If you go into the holding areas, you'll find a flagon of water. Proper fresh water. If you get the chance, fill your canteen.'

When we returned to the flagon to fill up, we found that the water had changed to the disgusting wood-marinade drawn from the well. The bastards had obviously seen me or heard me mentioning it. It is strange how, when you are confined to a very restricted environment, tiny things like the question of water loom large and make a huge difference to your thinking and your motivations.

I was surprised how upset I was at being eliminated on day seventeen in eighth place. As I came off set and into the holding area, my gaze was snagged by this amaz- ingly posh, gleaming toilet in its own prefabricated hut.

'Oh, my word!' I said to my handler. 'Look at those posh toilets over there. Who are they for?'

'Er, those are the same toilets that you saw and commented on when you came in a couple of weeks ago.'

That was when I realised how radically my perception of my surroundings had changed during my confine- ment. When I'd entered the set seventeen days earlier, I thought they were the grottiest, most disgusting toilets I'd ever seen; I would never have used them even if you'd paid me. After two and a half weeks of sleeping on a grate, rocking Sir Mo to sleep, being subjected to trials like Stage Fright, the Royal Tournament and the Rancid Rotisserie (I was excused Chambers of Horror on medical grounds) and the dunny that resembled Dante's fifth circle of Hell, the toilet in the holding area had gone from 'Eugh!' to 'Wow!'

From this fluorescent-lightbulb moment, I realised that I am an adaptable and robust survivor. Even if scarcely a life-changing experience, *I'm a Celebrity* ... made me realise that I can tolerate hardship better than I thought. When Armageddon comes and we are reduced to hunting for rats with sticks, I'll be just fine; I'll see the upside.

Not all my fellow contestants dealt with their time on set as well as me. Tears were shed over missed children. I missed my daughters but the only tears I shed were on my birthday, 24 November; I felt lonely not to be able to spend it with my family. But I never thought: *I can't deal with this, I want to go home.* I just cracked on with it.

I look back on *I'm a Celebrity* ... with great affection. I made some new friends and I think that it brought me to the attention of a completely new demographic. But I would soon discover how it helped prepare me for a real-life, real-world incarceration.

21

SURVIVAL SKILLS

IT WAS THE end of 2021, when Covid seemed to have peaked. The economy was on the move. It was time to get out of bed and re-engage. I was looking forward to getting properly back into performing for audiences again.

I was due to sing in a three-concert gig aboard a cruise ship during a twelve-day cruise to the Canaries and back, taking in Tenerife and Lanzarote. I love cruises. This one sounded like a fun job and I'd be back in time to help Louise with our house move from Dean House, Wilmslow, to a secluded farmhouse we'd bought on a hillside above Congleton on the River Dane in east Cheshire. The grounds of our farmhouse had enough room for our exotic menagerie of animals.

When I moved into Dean House, I was surrounded by rolling fields. Over the years, various car-dependent, medium density housing developments had encroached,

257

obliterating the fields with a security-gated development of over-clean-looking *Truman Show*-esque
identikit properties. It had become time to move on. A
few days at sea folded in luxury singing to an audience
excited to be on holiday would set me up perfectly for
the house move.

Dave, my assistant, a sound engineer, a musical direct-
or, an ensemble of musicians and I boarded the ship
together in Southampton one chilly day in December. All
went well until the day before I was due to leave the ship
and fly home, when we docked in Lisbon. Under
Portuguese law, everyone on board had to take a Covid
test. As someone whose leitmotif has been getting ill, I
suppose it was stupid of me to have imagined that Mother
Nature wouldn't seize on the opportunity of a pandemic
to have a shot at me. Being a lightning rod of ill health, I
was the only one of my group to test positive.

Immediately, I was escorted from my beautiful and
luxurious suite and taken below deck to – shall we say
– cosier, less cluttered quarters, quarters more reminis-
cent of a prison cell, where I sat thinking, *This could only
happen to me.*

My phone rang.

'I'm very sorry, Mr Watson. As you have tested positive
for Covid, you will have to spend ten days in isolation.
We think we have cleared it with the Portuguese

authorities that you can stay on board. We will soon be heading back to Southampton via Cádiz.'

I asked many questions, including whether they could put me in a better room.

'I'm afraid not, Mr Watson. You are confined to the isolation ward. We will do our best to look after you. Enjoy the rest of your cruise.'

One hour later, I took another call, from the same person.

'The Portuguese authorities have informed us that anyone testing positive for Covid must disembark and check in to a specially designated Covid hotel.'

'You mean, you are going to kick me off the ship?'

'I'm afraid so, Mr Watson.'

'But I'm in an isolation ward in a part of the ship dedicated to Covid passengers.'

'I'm sorry, Mr Watson. Those are the rules.'

'How does that make sense? I mean, let's imagine Portugal was my house. A taxi draws up outside carrying a bloke with a deadly illness. Do I bring him inside until he feels better? No. I'd send him away in the taxi. I wouldn't want him anywhere near my house.'

'I'm sorry, Mr Watson, we have to abide by the Portuguese authorities' ruling on the matter.'

However, Portugal soon sensibly changed its mind and decided it didn't want me after all. I was allowed to remain on board, albeit in the isolation ward. At least the food was good. I'd heard horror stories about people in similar situations – albeit not on board a luxury cruise ship, to be clear – being abandoned or forgotten about and left to starve.

I rang Dave.

'Next time you are passing the dining room, can you grab a set of cutlery and bring it to me? I'm not keen on this flimsy plastic cutlery. Thanks, Dave.'

A couple of hours later, Dave crept into the isolation ward and passed me a gleaming metal knife, fork and spoon.

That evening, the cruise ship slipped her moorings and thrummed south. When we docked in Cádiz the following morning, my phone rang.

'I'm sorry to have to inform you, Mr Watson, that Spanish law dictates that you must disembark the ship and go to a Covid hotel.'

Two men appeared wearing rubber suits. They each carried a cylinder spray like you'd use to spread weed killer over your garden. As I was escorted off the ship, one man walked in front of me spraying the air and the other walked behind me doing the same thing.

Jeez, I thought, *I've never seen anything like this.* It was like being in *ET*. When I saw the ambulance waiting on the quayside, white-coat fever began to rise. *What's wrong with me? Am I about to die?*

Nervously, I climbed aboard, and was driven to a hotel in Cádiz.

Cádiz. Even the name sounds like a prison. I expect it is twinned with Alcatraz. As I entered the lobby, the woman at reception leapt backwards as if I were radioactive.

'Go into the lift on the left.' She pointed vaguely towards the interior of the hotel.

'Here?'

'Sí . . . Floor five. Five!'

I ascended to the fifth floor. The receptionist, meanwhile, took a different lift and was waiting for me when I got out. She placed my door key on the floor and retreated. As I let myself into my room, she said: 'No leave. No answer. Go stay.'

Let's say my room wasn't the type that I'm used to on foreign tours. Sparse and impersonal, it felt like someone had died in it.

Ten minutes later, I got another call from reception.

'You need to stay in the room until you test negative for Covid. You can order whatever you want. You'll find a menu in the room. When you hear a knock at the door for delivery, please wait thirty seconds before opening. Thank you. Enjoy your stay.'

Enjoy your fucking stay! What day are we going to the beach?

I took in the extensive facilities of my room: desk, chair and bed that were *that* close to being landfill, and a soulless colour scheme. The main furniture was air, but not fresh. The windows were sealed and fastened with screws. The 'air con' was supplied by a fan in a corner that slowly twirled recycled air. *Well*, I thought, *no one will be coming into my room for at least a week, and when I'm gone, who cares.*

The survival skills and adaptability that I discovered while I was trying to get out of the hospital after my second operation, and which were developed and honed while on *I'm a Celebrity ... Get Me Out of Here!*, came into their own. I could hardly order a chisel and screwdriver on room service, so, producing the cruise ship cutlery, I began meticulously peeling away the sealant around the window frame. That took one day. On the second day, once again using the knife, I carefully undid every screw around the edge of the frame. That took several hours. There is always one screw that eludes you. It took me the best part of five hours to get the final, badly burred screw out. Its head had been damaged such that the knife was almost useless. Eventually I succeeded. As I yanked the entire window and its frame out of the wall, the breeze rushed in and I breathed in fresh lungfuls for the first time in three days. The sense of freedom and achievement made me feel like I had climbed Mount Everest.

Having already been quarantined for two days on the ship, I calculated that I had eight nights left. I managed to fill three more days by filming a video diary, as well as staring at the ceiling and looking out of the window.

My friend Ged Mason very kindly tried to organise a private jet to fly me home. The authorities were having none of it.

The phone rang.

'Er, unfortunately, Mr Watson, it's not three more days,' said the man from the shipping company that had organised my travel arrangements. 'It's five more days. According to Spanish law, the two days you spent quarantined on the ship don't count.'

'You told me the days on the ship did count.'

'I'm sorry, there is nothing we can do about it. It's the law.'

'This is just a money-making racket, isn't it? This is just a way of getting people into a hotel during a period when people still aren't travelling much. People are being held captive indoors for days on end, having to eat the hotel food and then being charged for it. It's a rip-off.'

I put the phone down, sat down on the bed and thought, I'm a Celebrity . . . *has nothing on this*. It felt like solitary confinement, a test of character. I was also feel-ing stressed to the eyeballs.

Then something came into my sight. I saw what looked like a kaleidoscope of zig-zag coloured lines moving about and closing in. *What the . . .?*

I lay back on the bed and cried: 'My life is just one disaster after another! People are going to say, "Jesus Christ, is he ever all right?"'

Even if I placed my hands over my eyes. I could still see this kaleidoscope of coloured zig-zagging lines. *Of all the places I could choose to die! Why here?* I thought. *I don't want to die here alone in this room, not in Cádiz! In the Covid hotel!*

My PTSD, along with a real sense of hopelessness, had kicked in.

I rang Tara.

'Calm down,' she said. 'Tell me what's happening.'

I explained to her my symptoms, the coloured lines that shifted about in my gaze like a kaleidoscope.

'It sounds like low blood pressure. You need to take some more cortisol. You sound really stressed.'

'Did someone say "stress"? Are you kidding?'

I went through the story of how an enjoyable concert tour ended up with me, my luggage and a set of finest cruise ship cutlery in a fifth-floor hotel room in Cádiz with a gaping hole in the wall.

'So, yes,' I said, 'I suppose that, what with all that going on, and having Covid symptoms and thinking about moving house, you could say I'm under a bit of stress.'

'Yes, yes, quite,' said Tara. 'Look, Russell, you need fluids and sugar too. Ask for a sugary drink and some chocolate.'

I rang room service. As soon as I drank the sugary drink and ate the chocolate and took my hydrocortisone, I began to feel better. The kaleidoscope dissolved and I realised that I might yet live to see another day.

With three days left, the time had come to prepare for my journey home. A certain amount of online form-filling was necessary. The company that was looking after me told me not to worry, that it would sort everything out. 'We'll take care of everything, Mr Watson,' they assured me.

Later that afternoon, the phone rang.

'Hello, Mr Watson. Are you still testing positive? We have just heard from the government that Boris Johnson has changed the rules. You cannot re-enter the United Kingdom unless and until you test negative.'

The irony was that I wasn't locked in. At any point, I could have got up, left the room, walked down the stairs, waved *hola! hola!* to reception, who wouldn't have had a clue who I was, and slipped out into Cádiz. Nothing was stopping me, apart from the law.

I noticed that the red line of the Covid test had got thinner. When I first arrived, there was a big thick line.

With two days left of my 'prison sentence' in Cádiz, there was a knock on the door. A quietly spoken gentleman walked in carrying a suitcase and introduced himself as 'Jesús'.

He tested me negative and said he'd contact me the next day. We began to chat. It turned out that he knew who I was and that one of his family had seen me perform in London.

'This is a blessing from above,' I said. 'Someone called Jesus comes along, tests me negative and I'm finally on my way home. I'm saved!'

When I got to the airport, a curt gentleman at check-in asked: 'Have you got your form?'

'It's been filled in online.'

'You need it with you.'

'I haven't got it. It's been filled in online.'

'What's your name?'

'Russell Watson.'

'You cannot travel without the form, Mr Watson.'

I rang my shipping company and, after much to-ing and fro-ing, ended up engaging a special services person to help me manually fill in the right form.

By the time I finally made it back home, some week

and a half later than originally planned, I found that Louise had moved house from Wilmslow to our new home in Congleton all by herself, with no input from me.

Thankfully, the shipping company paid my hotel bill. As for my window renovations, they were never mentioned again.

*　*　*

My handiwork in Cádiz whetted my appetite for further DIY experimentation. When Louise and I eventually moved into our farmhouse in Congleton, we found a long-neglected outdoor pool. Filthy, it was filled with black water. Several swimming pool maintenance companies quoted us five-figure sums to have it refurbished.

'If you didn't already own a pool, that is what a new one would cost,' said Louise. 'Let's fill it in and build a tennis court.'

No.

I did my homework. I researched everything there is to know about swimming pool refurbishment. I then rang Chris Lee, a pal who is also Louise's equine dental technician. Over nine weeks in summer 2022, I became DIY Superman. Chris and I emptied and cleaned out the pool, sanded it down and repainted it. We also dug out and cleaned the pumps. Result: a brand new-looking pool for about £200. Meanwhile, I was juggling a full programme of concerts while helping Louise bottle-feed two cade (orphaned) lambs and playing out a rescue-fantasy dragon-slaying act in saving a couple of chickens from the overzealous attentions of our cockerel.

22

A STAGE IN LIFE

In 2022, I was offered the role of Billy Flynn, the criminal defence lawyer in the musical *Chicago*: eight shows a week for three months, a heavy-duty load. Ten years earlier, I would never have dreamt of doing such a thing. I doubt I could have sustained it. In 2022, however, I had reached a stage in life, and an understanding of how to manage my fitness, hormonal balance, mortality and voice, that made me think, *This isn't just me singing and acting in a musical and performing eight shows a week; it represents a new challenge that I want to take on.* I had never done anything like this before – it felt like a personal mountain to climb.

Being both a good mimic and a perfectionist, I wanted to get Flynn's accent, vowels and resonance exactly right. I didn't want to go on stage talking like I was from *Noo Yark*, for example; that's no good. Chicago – Chicaygo – has its own accent, a slightly nasal whine with a shift of the 'th' sound to a 'd'. 'That thing over there' becomes 'dat ding over dere'.

The challenge I had taken on was compounded when four weeks' rehearsal time shrank to two. (The original cast had five weeks.) A process that began with me and the musical director sitting in a room poring over the book ended up a fortnight later with me in full costume, hair and make-up stepping out on a stage in front of a ticket-paying audience and a full orchestra. Not only was there the shock of the Liverpool Empire, an expansive 2,700-seater, being rammed for all eight nights – a wonderful sight to behold from the stage, of course – but also the shock of having a full company of dancers and actors on stage with me. Having human beings moving around me while I performed felt completely unlike what I was used to, which is me standing on my own in mid-stage and singing. I'd been on the stage with other performers, of course, duetting and as part of the concert production of *Kristina*, but, whereas *Kristina* was almost like a full-blown opera in concept, subject matter and construction, *Chicago* felt completely different – so much was going on and all at tempo. With an entire cast of people around me with their own roles to play, I felt the pressure was on, which I enjoyed.

As soon as I walked on, the audience roared.

'Is everybody here?' I began. 'Is everybody ready?' I turned to the band. 'Hit it!'

The first performances went well. They say in musicals it takes one month to figure out your role. Sure enough, by week four I felt my confidence growing. In the show, there was more ad-libbing and dialogue than I was used to. The courtroom scene at the end when Roxie Hart is tried for the murder of her lover but Flynn gets her off took a lot of work to get right. I felt physically drained at the end of each performance.

Chicago was the first time I had played the rogue. Flynn, a shady lawyer, isn't exactly the bad guy, but he certainly isn't the good guy. Everyone has their own view of what kind of character he is. Different actors have lent different interpretations: some have made him light-hearted and jovial, others, darker, unpleasant and almost gangster-like. I saw him as a self-absorbed narcissist fantasist driven only by money who is trying to wind everyone around his little finger in order to get what he wants. He comes up with ways of manipulating and manoeuvring others. He is interested neither in love nor the women around him. I drew on no real-life inspiration, just my own imagination. None of my lawyer friends could provide a role model. Flynn may be a narcissist but at least he has charisma.

271

Chicago taught me at least two things: one, never accept a two-week rehearsal time, and two, be 110 per cent sure of being 'off book', a theatre word that means that you have memorised your lines and no longer need to carry your script on stage. It took me until the end of my first week in Liverpool to get off book. *Chicago* also showed me that, while hormones are a big part of your character, other things like determination and willpower are important too. That was a reassuring and validating thing for me to understand, having felt so reliant on balancing replacement hormones. Turned out that I was more than just the product of my medicine cupboard, more than merely the sum of different pharmaceuticals that I have to take every day.

When my run came to an end, I felt proud. I'd done it! I saw it as a massive triumph, a mountain climbed, another string to my bow.

* * *

The performing arts are going through a general crisis, especially in my line. Opportunities to entertain live audiences on television shows are becoming increasingly scarce. Very few programmes these days support live artistry. The mainstays these days are celebrity

shows such as *Ant & Dec's Saturday Night Takeaway,*
Jonathan Ross and *The Graham Norton Show.* Even then,
the guest talent tends to be modern, on-trend bands or
solo pop artists plugging a new album. You rarely see a
megastar like Elton John, Rod Stewart or Paul McCartney.
In previous decades, there was more airtime available
for showcasing singing talent.

The majority of live music entertainment shows are
talent contests aimed at finding the Next Big Thing.
Whenever I see young talent coming through on these
shows, I recognise the look on their faces as they stare
dazed and blinking into the headlights of the celebrity
bandwagon hurtling towards them. I know what it feels
like to be desperate for your few minutes of fame; I
know what it feels like to walk on stage thinking, *This is*
my one opportunity.

Once new talent is discovered, you rarely hear about
them again. Next Big Things soon become Previous
Small Things – that's if they are lucky. Most of them are
forgotten about or consigned to the dustbin of history as
celebrity roadkill. Mad, really. There seems to be little
interest in sustaining talent or cultivating the arts in
general. It saddens me that many artists don't get past
first base.

I have enjoyed my own experience of TV talent shows,
however. In late 2022 I was invited to compete on *The*

Masked Singer, the musical reality game show that origi-
nated in South Korea. Celebrities put on elaborate masks
or head-to-toe costumes that conceal their identities and
then sing a song. A panel of celebrity judges tries to
guess the identity of the performer based on clues that
the singer drops. The audience then votes on who they
like the most. The singer with the fewest votes in each
round is eliminated and unmasked.

It was taken terribly seriously. I was placed under
strict rules of confidentiality and given a code name. Not
even my family knew. Before I arrived at the studio, I
had to pull over and get changed in the back of a car.
Wearing a T-shirt emblazoned with 'Do Not Speak to
Me', I pulled on gloves so no one saw my hands, socks
to conceal my ankles, and a balaclava and helmet with
visor to hide the shape of my head. In the studio, I had to
dress up in a giant combat cockroach outfit that weighed
a tonne. I would have blended in perfectly at a fancy
dress party themed *A Bug's Life* meets *Gladiator.* I sang
'Go the Distance', which Michael Bolton performs over
the end credits of Disney's animated film *Hercules.*

Welcome to the surreal contours of a life in celebrity.
I've done a few things, television shows and performances, but after this one even I thought, *Well that was a
bit different!* Dressing up as a giant cockroach was quite
fun and provided an opportunity to sing and raise my

profile on national television. It was fantastic to be part of one of the big, shiny-floor specials again. The production on the show was second to none.

I ended up losing to a giant kangaroo.

When I finally extricated myself from my giant cockroach outfit and set off for home, my daughter Rebecca rang barely able to contain her laughter.

'I'm crying laughing, Dad,' she shouted. 'I can't believe what you have just done!'

'Welcome to the shifting imperatives of my artistic career,' I said. 'Actually, I quite enjoyed it. It was strangely liberating.'

Yet I still yearned to get back to singing classical operatic arias. Covid had decimated the opportunities to do so, but the pandemic also brought about an unexpected dividend.

23

YOU'VE BEEN A LOVELY AUDIENCE

PATRICK MCGUIGAN WAS correct when he said that the voice deteriorates with age. But I'm glad that I didn't take him too seriously. I pushed on and followed my own star. While Covid was a disaster for many performance artists, for me it was an unexpected blessing in a way that I could never have imagined. It came at a time in my life when many singers begin to wear their voices out. So often, classical singers, paranoid about how long their career will last, try to pack too much in and risk damaging their voices so that their paranoia becomes self-fulfilling. The enforced rest that the pandemic imposed on my voice – six months off singing altogether, my longest silence, and almost eighteen months off touring – had literally worked wonders. My control is better than ever. I can pull things around. I can flit out of full voice and into falsetto and back. I can turn the volume down to a pin-drop and rock things up to deafening.

The way my career is managed has also changed, and is very different from those early days, back in the early 2000s. Now I don't need someone to negotiate a tour deal for me. I know how it works. Rather than handing over control (and cash) to a shiny agent who will produce a cheque at the end of it (minus costs), Louise and I do everything ourselves. I know what catering for thirty costs, and what a seven-ton van costs to hire. I know how much the venue and band will cost. If I need a small orchestra, Louise will call our fixer, who will arrange all the string players and professional musicians. We do all the scene-setting ourselves, including lighting. It's like a cottage industry, where I get to work with people I know and like, who will do a good job. It is more work but the profit is greater and the satisfaction is immense. I'm producer, manager and product.

We vary production costs, depending on the size of venue and whether I have an orchestra or not. Costs and production values move along a sliding scale. Even in quite small venues, you can make a similar profit to what you'd hope to get in a big metropolitan theatre.

A venue that seats six hundred, like a small church, doesn't have to require massive outlay. I just tuck my iPad under my arm and walk in with Rob, my driver, whose day job is farming. He toddles along behind me holding my suit jacket. It's a far cry from gristle in suits calling out, 'Mr Watson is coming through!' And, actually, much better for my ego. Limos picking me up from Trump International Hotel were fun, but they are not my choice of reality.

When using local artists, I try to research them as thoroughly as possible, and make sure they are who they say they are and can do the job with minimal rehearsal time. Mike Moran and I will comb through YouTube clips, videos and biographies to get a feel for a musician or guest artist.

I believe I have found a happy middle ground, steering between triumph and tribulation, where stuff seems to come my way without having to force the issue. For many of us, security trumps dream fulfilment any day. Most of us worry more about losing money than missing out on a gain. But having experienced extremes of financial gain and pain, I've learnt that, if you are not counting the money, you are not in business. After years of muddling through, I think I've worked out how to limit the downside and allow myself a shot at carrying on living the dream.

While I'm often mistaken for a powder keg of emotion, I like to think that, when it comes to all aspects of performing, I have the necessary drive, single-mindedness and discipline. I rarely switch off. I'm always

meticulous in my pre-concert preparations: I watch my
diet, avoid booze, stay fit and, above all, keep relaxed.
Afterwards, as soon as the stage lights go down and the
audience files home, I'm out with the calculator or scroll-
ing through ticket sales for the next gig. How many tickets have we sold here? How many there? I need to sell
another fifteen in St Albans. Right, get me a radio slot for
the St Albans area and let's shift those tickets. How are
we doing in Blackburn?

An agent I worked with once said, 'Russell, you are
unlike any other artist.'

'Why?'

'You just won't stop.'

To me, money is a by-product. Yes, it's important – you
can't keep doing the job and putting on concerts without
it – but nothing beats seeing a packed-out venue, going
on stage to belt it out and getting a standing ovation. I
can't put a price on that.

*   *   *

I suppose I've also always enjoyed being a musical
chameleon, collecting new colours as I mature. I like to
cross borders and explore different vocal realms where
classicists are either unwilling or unable to tread. I see
no reason why I shouldn't sing 'Livin' on a Prayer' by

Bon Jovi, in the style it was intended to be performed in. Or 'Circle of Life' or 'Nature Boy' or songs from the golden era of Hollywood musicals. Ask me nicely and I might even sing the telephone directory in almost any style and key. I sing musical theatre, I sing pop music, I sing soul music.

Early-ish in my career, when I was mainly known as a classical crossover artist, Ian Wright, the former Arsenal football player turned television presenter, had me on his Christmas special on ITV. At rehearsal, I grabbed the microphone and sang 'The Christmas Song' by Nat King Cole.

Chestnuts roasting on an open fire . . .

When I'd finished, Ian came over, mouth wide open, and said, 'I wasn't expecting that!'

'What?'

'I thought you were an opera singer.'

'What were you expecting?'

'I dunno! Not that!'

I think he was expecting [operatic voice]: *Chestnu-u-u-uts rrrroasting on an o-o-o-pen fire . . .*

Fundamentally, I'm a recording artist. I'm also, if you like, classical music's pimp. People come up to me and say, 'Oh yeah, you're that opera singer, aren't you? I don't really like opera.'

'What opera don't you like?'

'Er ... I can't really name any. I just don't like that singing.'

'What singing?'

'Er, the big singing. The *Ah-ah-ah-ah!* stuff.'

'What big singing? Tell me what you don't like. It's not all big singing.'

'I don't like classical music.'

You have to give stuff a chance. It's stupid to dismiss something that has been formulated and refined over hundreds of years just because you've heard one or two things that aren't you. What I hope to encourage people to do when I choose songs to perform on stage or record for an album is give it a chance.

There must be millions in this country who, until the arrival of big classical music radio stations, probably never listened to classical music. Now, many of them say, 'Oh, I put on Classic FM all the time. I find it relaxing', or 'I chuck on a Spotify "classical chillout" readymade playlist', whereas previously they would probably neither have thought about it nor admitted to liking classical. It is all about giving people the chance.

When my grandmother listened to Led Zeppelin, she said, 'Rubbish!' When I listen to my daughters' choice of contemporary pop music in the car, I quite like some of it. They have compiled me a playlist of tracks that I would never have got round to listening to had they not introduced me to them. I'm not claiming to be down with the kids, but we could all do with being pointed in a new direction now and then.

Left to my own devices, I tend to still stick on Elton John or The Jam. *All Mod Cons*, The Jam's most exciting album, conjures so many memories, whisking me back to childhood days kicking a football around with my pals in Prince's Park in Irlam or jamming along in my bedroom with my Hofner semi-acoustic guitar that I now deeply regret selling. Life and the world seemed less complicated then. Perhaps social media, with its unending stream of misery, has contributed to my yearning for nostalgia. Don't worry, I'm not about to say, 'Things sounded better on vinyl!' I'm just saying we can hold on to things we like without closing our minds to the possibility of discovering something new to enjoy or riding the shifts in our personal tastes that makes the awful suddenly start sounding interesting and then brilliant.

I often hear: 'I love *you*, Russell, but I'm not a fan of classical music.'

'Have you ever been to my concerts?'

'No.'

'I think I might be able to change your mind.'

I get great pleasure from people who come up to me

283

and say, 'You weren't really my thing, but I came along with my wife/husband/friend and I really enjoyed your show.'

Nothing turns a rock fan into a classical album-buyer as easily as 'Nessun dorma'; nothing turns a bloke with a vest into a concert-goer so much as 'O sole mio'; nothing turns a bingo nut into a believer more than 'Volare'. If people begin by playing the man, I can generally persuade them to play the ball too. Fortunately, other than on social media, I've never heard anyone say, 'I dislike you, Russell, but I do like your music.'

I like putting on songs that make me feel melancholic and teary. I'm not ashamed to admit to a good wallow now and then. If I want to feel really heavy-hearted, I'll grab a box of tissues and stick on my favourite classical pieces, like Intermezzo from *Cavalleria Rusticana*, Pietro Mascagni's one-act opera, but it has to be the version with the organ playing in it from the actual opera. This piece was my grandmother's favourite.

Or I'll pop on a bit of John Barry. One particular track is Barry's adaptation of the eighteenth variation of Sergei Rachmaninoff's *Rhapsody on a Theme of Paganini*. Oh, my word! It always hits the spot.

Once Mascagni and Barry go on, it's game over. Everything else stops.

Another piece that affects me immediately, although I can't for the life of me explain why, is 'The Crisis' by Ennio Morricone, part of the soundtrack of the Italian film *The Legend of 1900*. Played on a de-tuned piano, it just goes *bloung-bloung-bloung-bloung, bloung-bloung-bloung-bloung* all the way through with a couple of variations on the chords. When the strings come in, I go to pieces.

There is nothing like a bracing dose of self-pity while listening to Barry and Morricone, two master manipulators in music.

In 2001, I met John Barry. It was perhaps a measure of my fame at the time that he and Don Black wrote a song for me. This was during the heady second-album days on Long Beach Island. I drove down to visit John. His estate in Oyster Bay, New York state, was a beautiful property with a typical American ranch-type spread in the middle. His piano room had a magnificent Steinway standing centre stage, and walls lined with bookshelves of music. Dotted around the house were statuettes. As John and I chatted, I asked, 'What are all these statue things all over the house?'

'Oh, they are Grammys, Russell.'

He said it in such an unassuming fashion, almost as though he were embarrassed that he had so many. Maybe that's why they weren't all together in a beautifully lit cabinet. That's certainly what I would be doing with them if I had won them!

It was interesting to observe how John and his wife Laurie operated as a team. She seemed to exert quite an influence. An attractive lady, she was very pragmatic about everything and she was clearly very supportive of John. I could see that she was the driving force. I remember thinking how it must be fantastic to have a partner like that in your life. You hear of so many relationships in the music industry that are opposite, that break down because of pressures and demands. Their relationship, however, seemed very strong. All these years later, I feel like Louise gives me that support and we are very strong as a result, far greater than the sum of our parts.

John and I met again in London. We went to a studio where John played the song that he had composed for me. I quite liked it but it didn't strike me as the greatest.

In what, with hindsight, was probably the most idiotic move of my life, I turned down John Barry. I cannot believe I have just typed those words. *The singer who turned down John Barry.* Along with selling my Hofner semi-acoustic guitar and losing my copy of the *NME* featuring me and Shaun Ryder, my greatest regret is that I didn't walk back into the studio and say, 'John,

I love it. It leaps off the page. There are a couple of things. Maybe we can change this or lighten that . . .?' I needed a Louise figure or a Laurie figure to knock sense into me.

Or perhaps it was some sort of imposter syndrome. Maybe something deep down in my brain couldn't quite compute that John Barry had really written a song for *me*. John's offer was a genuinely meant offer for us to work together. Even today, I have very few celebrity friends. In purely professional terms, that is probably to my detriment. I've met and worked with some of the biggest names but I have never tried to build relationships, perhaps for fear of being perceived as trying to ride on coat tails.

I have always been ambivalent about the celebrity freemasonry that you see manifesting in the Hades that is light entertainment events and on red carpets. There are some who assiduously work that circuit. They blunt the hard edges, shimmy from one opinion to another, say what they imagine others want to hear, allow themselves to be seduced by proximity to celebrity and power, and generally behave like well-oiled weathervanes. Some have done very well and have a body of industry pals who scratch each other's backs. But I feel uncomfortable and intimidated. I find myself overthinking and trimming my conversation, which isn't me. Whereas with my pals from Salford, I can say what I want and no one is offended. My ambition is to spread the joy, make a few quid and not sell my soul.

I wonder what happened to John and Don's song. Maybe another singer had more sense than me. Maybe it is sitting in a drawer somewhere. Even if it came to light, singing it now wouldn't be the same without John. He died in 2011.

*   *   *

I suppose when I think about it, I just still feel like the ordinary bloke in Salford that I began life as. I have to pinch myself when I think that, in my twenty-five years or so as a recording artist, I've had the honour to perform in front of presidents, kings and emperors. I even performed before Pope John Paul II in a concert at The Vatican. The joy of being asked for a signed CD by His Holiness (for which a blessing and thank you letter came by post in an envelope with an amazing wax seal a few weeks later) was only counteracted by me confusing the word 'Pontiff' with 'Plaintiff' in a TV interview after the performance. This was at the time of my legal battles with my then management – so the press had a field day with my unfortunate malapropism!

In September 2022, just six days after the death of the Queen, I was honoured to be invited by Sky Sports to sing 'God Save the King', in one of the first televised football games since the Queen's death – Preston North End v Burnley. The atmosphere in the stadium was fever pitch. Everyone rose to their feet. Even now I can feel the goose bumps. The way everyone behaved that day reflected how they felt about the Queen.

In fact, some of the proudest moments of my career – and life – have involved the royal family. I was honoured to perform at an event at Buckingham Palace, in the garden, for Prince Philip's ninetieth birthday. I sang a few songs, including 'Jerusalem'. It was awesome. But the most special part of it all was the moment when, looking up at Buckingham Palace before me, I caught sight of a curtain twitching at one of the windows, only to reveal the Queen, stood there, watching the performance from above. *Wow! What an honour,* I remember thinking to myself.

After the performance, the Duke walked over to me. I was still holding my microphone.

'What's that for?' he said. 'You don't need a microphone! They can hear you in space!'

We both chuckled.

My wife and I entered the living room.

'Who are you?' he said to Louise.

'I'm Russell's wife, Your Royal Highness,' Louise replied.

'You must be deaf living with him!' the Duke said back.

'Pardon?' quipped Louise.

The joke was not lost on the Duke, who laughed and then shuffled on.

A year later, I was honoured to perform in a concert at Buckingham Palace to celebrate the Diamond Jubilee. And I have also been privileged to perform at Windsor Castle for the then Prince Charles and Duchess of Cornwall. I have been an ambassador for the Prince's Trust for over twenty years.

But one of my top royal encounters was in Japan. I was performing a set of classical repertoire in the Imperial Palace. Afterwards one of the Emperor's aides came running over to me. 'The Emperor has requested you for dinner!' I'm looking round the room; there's two and a half thousand people in the room, and I'm thinking I'm just going to be popped down at one of the tables and have something to eat. No. I was pulled up a chair right next to the Emperor of Japan. The first thought that came into my mind was, 'What do I say to the Emperor of Japan?' I sat down. The Emperor looked at me, and the first thing that he said was 'Which football team do you support?'

'Manchester United,' I replied.

'Ah, like the Urawa Reds!'

'Just like the Urawa Reds, in fact I actually sang on the pitch at the Urawa Reds game the other day.'

Well, that was it. The ice was well and truly broken and we clicked and chatted away happily for the rest of the night. It turned out that the Emperor was a great football fan too. We also discussed our shared love of wines and champagnes.

At the end of the evening everyone stood up as the Emperor and Empress prepared to leave. Instinctively I went to shake hands with the Emperor – and he reciprocated. Afterwards, when the Emperor had left the room, an aide ran over to me with a look of disbelief on his face.

'Do you know what has just happened?' he said.

'Hmm, no!'

'The Emperor has shaken your hand. No one ever shakes the Emperor's hand. That is a great honour!'

Blimey, I thought. From the back street working men's clubs of the North West, to hanging out with the Emperor and shaking his hand. What next?

* * *

While my voice is at its highest level of excellence, and I believe I am singing better than ever, how much longer can it last? Ten years? Those ten years will fly past. I hope they don't include any more health scares, unpleasant shocks or acts of God.

As I mature and drift apart from the industry in its formal guise, I find myself more and more in tune with my humanity and mortality. In some ways, that is a positive development, but I dislike the idea that one day, I, my children, my wife and all the people whom I love will not be around. When you have been through shit like I have, this idea looms larger than in perhaps most people's minds. In my early twenties, I laughed at death. Now, I take it seriously. Certain things I will not do, like get on a horse or motorcycle or jump out of an aeroplane, even with a parachute on. Not because I'm scared; it's just that I value life too much to take chances and I feel I have used up most of my chances.

I'm still in good shape and feel good. Before I started singing classical music, I looked nothing like I do today. My upper body development is down to singing, breathing and technique. Swimming takes priority over all other forms of exercise. Every day, I swim between 1,200 and 1,500 metres in one go.

The process of regeneration that I started in 2014 when I went back to see Patrick goes deeper than simply a career refurb with a few scatter cushions here and a conversation piece or two there. It's more modern. It's a process, an endless debate and a negotiation. I am in a state of constant reinvention, continual revolution, a simple optimist searching for truths. I'm a multi-tasking, easy-listening evangelist of continual readjustment, a seeker of enlightenment who has transcended ego and vanity. Well, that's what I tell the mirror.

In Congleton, I've traded the limo ride down Fifth Avenue from Trump International to Times Square for bracing dog walks in an anorak across the hills with a copy of *The Wild Flowers of East Cheshire* in my pocket. I no longer have a bucket list, nor do I need to fill my life with excitement, thrills and spills. I've done that. I just want steadily to tootle on down the highway of life, alternating between fast and slow lanes. I don't need to sit on the hard shoulder and I only want occasional visits to the service station. I certainly don't expect to venture off road. Occasional frustrations with the music industry aside, in my heart of hearts I don't care if my albums never make it to number one. I don't care if I never fill another arena or stadium. I'm happy doing the venues I do, working in theatres and on television. I cannot tell you how happy I am not to have to think, *Oh my God, will I work next year?* I have found my proper place in the universe.

I don't carry my gongs, baubles, accolades and

standing ovations around with me in a suitcase. I do what I do, and it is what it is. Sometimes I feel like I've taken the scenic route to get where I am, but that's life! I still nurse an inner belief that, if I keep moving forward, then at some point something extraordinary may catalyse.

Rich? Poor? I've been both and I don't really care. Let me tell you, you can have all the money in the world and the finest cars, yachts and jets to get you around it, but they don't make you happy. They don't stop you doubting yourself. They don't stop you feeling low. Just because one person has money and another person doesn't, there is no rule that says the first should feel great and the second should feel shit. Money and possessions aren't just beside the point; they are striving for the wrong point. Sometimes, they exacerbate doubt and depression. You find yourself thinking, *I've got all this money and success, yet I'm still not happy. There must be something* really *wrong with me.* Money can also come between friends, which is ugly.

Once I stopped letting my career and the pressure to succeed get the better of me, my life, mindset and mental health improved dramatically. That sense of constantly feeling under pressure to do everything dissipated. I explored the grey middle ground between burnout and paranoia. It comes with age and realising that there are more important things. I look at my career now and think it is just that, my career, like a physical object that is parked outside the house waiting to be taken out for a run-about, or a piece in a very large board game. I love it. I love being on stage. I love singing. But I enjoy spending time with my wife and grown up daughters just as much as the stardom. I find that maintaining a simplicity and a bosky kind of natural anonymity at home in Congleton is far more gratifying than appearing on television or having my name in neon.

When Louise and I moved to Congleton, both of my daughters moved to Congleton too. They wanted to be closer to me. They need me. I need them. We see each other all the time, and I call them every day. I am a sounding board and a conduit. We have all been through a lot together. For a period of time they even became my protectors. After my second brain operation, if we were walking through a shopping centre and someone approached, my children kept them away. 'Our dad's not well.' Rebecca is 29, Hannah, 23. I need no one to tell me I'm a good dad. I can see that in my daughters. I have a completely different relationship with each one. With Hannah, deep and thoughtful, I have long discussions about all kinds of topics; Rebecca is more into movies, clothes, laughing, joking, Snapchat and silly videos. Both are musical; neither has done much about it. I should have liked them to play or sing but I'm no tiger parent. Instead of push-push-push, I've let them find their way, do their own thing. Rebecca works in the care sector; Hannah, in the NHS. My daughters and I have been through a lot together. We are probably closer as a result. If they have a problem or need advice, they always call.

I don't consider myself to be anything other than a normal bloke who sings. I like fitting in without being noticed. My celebrity is just the right size, shape and fit for me. I can go out and play Mr Normal Bloke without being mobbed. What gives me greatest satisfaction is when people come up to me and thank me for the joy and happiness that I have spread. That happens just enough to give me room to hang out and be myself, whoever that may be.

I hope people think that I've got this fabulous voice and sparkling personality that comes across in the music that I sing and the way I sing it, and that I'm easy to get along with and friendly to people who are friendly to me. I don't believe that anything fame and fortune have brought me has changed my outlook on human beings and life in general. I leave that to other celebrities and super stars. I wouldn't mind living in a two-up, two-down so long as I'm happy. Everything else is a bonus that I never thought I'd attain.

Looking back at my career after twenty-five years at the

sharp end of show business, I think I've worked hard, survived an improbable number of potentially killer knocks and more or less deserved what I've got. When I cast my mind back further still to the shop floor in Salford on £90 a week, and working the pubs and clubs at £70 a gig, I often turn and look outside the back door of my farmhouse above Congleton. As I stand there and admire the majestic sweep of hills washed with sunshine and crowned by the heath-capped summit of Bosley Cloud on the Cheshire/Staffordshire border, I gasp at the beauty and find that I can scarcely believe what I have achieved.